Faith without Honor
and dogs that can't hunt

Ben Hardister

Faith without Honor
and dogs that can't hunt

© 2014 by Ben Hardister

Published in cooperation with Next Step Books, P.O. Box 70271, West Valley City, Utah 84170

Scripture quotations marked KJV are taken from the Holy Bible, King James Version, Cambridge, 1769.

Scripture quotations marked NIV are taken from the Holy Bible, New International Version®, NIV®. Copyright © 1973, 1978, 1984, 2011 by Biblica, Inc.™ Used by permission of Zondervan. All rights reserved worldwide. www.zondervan.com The "NIV" and "New International Version" are trademarks registered in the United States Patent and Trademark Office by Biblica, Inc.™

Scripture quotations marked NLT are taken from the Holy Bible, New Living Translation, copyright ©1996, 2004, 2007 by Tyndale House Foundation. Used by permission of Tyndale House Publishers, Inc., Carol Stream, Illinois 60188. All rights reserved.

Scripture quotations marked NKJV are taken from the New King James Version®. Copyright © 1982 by Thomas Nelson, Inc. Used by permission. All rights reserved.

Cover design by Nick Delliskave

ISBN-13: 978-1-937671-21-1
ISBN-10: 1937671216

What People Are Saying About Ben Hardister and *Faith without Honor*

Ben is a man with words. Words like integrity, passion, no fear, and "Never say no to God's need!" He single-handedly rescued us when there was no one else. He's a man to be depended on, with or without money, because somehow he always gets what we need. He would give his last dollar to save a soul, and stand alone to defend the poor. He would search for a lost soul as if looking for gold. As the saying goes, "Many are called, but few are chosen." Ben is one of the chosen.

Roger Huang
Founder of San Francisco City Impact Ministry
Author of Chasing God

Ben Hardister is a unique man, gifted in so many ways. A true friend, a mentor, motivator, man of God with astounding biblical insight. A huge heart for the world, who has blessed multitudes by putting his money where his mouth is. Never afraid to meet a challenge and never afraid to challenge all of us to take leaps of faith to accomplish great things for God. Ben put up a significant amount of his personal money and had six others join him in the challenge to purchase the "Marine Property" in Calcutta, India for the School of Nursing. This was a huge $800,000 project. The "Magnificent 7" as I call them, came, saw and gave. Today the huge health care system reaching 100,000 patients a year has nursing care because of Ben. Thanks is never enough. The rewards of Ben's sacrifices will be measured in eternal worth. As Ben would say "God moves when you move." Ben has taken on the challenge to have God's blessing come down on all those that help to heal the open sore of the world. The world and the kingdom of God is a better place because of the giant footprint of faith and giving that Ben Hardister has left.

Wayne Francis, Ministry Representative
Calcutta Mercy Ministry, India

While serving in Venezuela as a missionary 18 years ago, I had the privilege of meeting Ben and Karen Hardister. Since the time we met we have partnered together to build drug rehab centers in Venezuela for more than five hundred kids. I have watched his passion for the lost as he helped to build an entire orphanage for the street kids of Mexico and most recently become a major partner in the building of a Teen Challenge center for girls in Cambodia. Through the eyes of men, Ben's view of giving to needs will separate the men from the boys. But through God's eyes, he tells us to have the faith of a child. Ben and Karen are some of the few people I met who have learned to trust God with a faith of a child, believing, trusting and holding God entirely to his promises. Nothing we hold here on earth is of any value except for the treasures that we store in heaven, Ben is the friend that you can always trust in not to tell you what you want to hear, but what you need to hear. As you read through the pages of this book I pray that God will give you the child-like faith that you can trust him for anything.

David Wagner
Seed One Ministry

When I think of Ben Hardister I think of 2 Corinthians 5-7, for we live by faith, not by sight. Ben exemplifies this faith in his daily walk. Ben's book shares how God can use the faith of a mustard seed to move mountains. Ben's faith and obedience shows biblical principles and how the Holy Spirit will use an individual to be a vessel to glorify God's Kingdom. *Faith without Honor*, is extremely encouraging and is a must read to hear true accounts of how God can use any one of us.

David Akers
Reverend, 15-year NFL Kicker, 6x Pro Bowler

Faith without Honor. What a fitting title for a book written by Benjamin Hardister. I have known and respected the ministry of Ben for more than 30 years. This book speaks to the heart of our spiritual consciousness. Insightful and challenging, this book is Benny. The manner in which this book is written is the same manner in which he ministered to the men at San Quentin Prison for over 10 years. Ben was and is a model of consistency and spiritual accountability. I have long hoped that he would share his story in written form about the redemptive power of Christ. After reading this book, I can only say how blessed I am to have encountered Benjamin Hardister on my journey. Benny is committed to Kingdom Principles and Benny "will hunt".

Chaplain Earl A. Smith, Sr.
Retired Chaplain
California State Prison, San Quentin
2000 National Correctional Chaplain of the Year

I have listened to the stories and experiences of Ben Hardister's life and it is a continuation of the Book of Acts. He challenges every believer to move from average to obedience. Stephen, Phillip and others were not apostles or pastors in scripture; they were simply church folks that believed God could use them to work miracles. I can honestly say Ben Hardister is genuine, unashamed, passionate and a soul winner.

Warning: If you read this book, you will have to throw away every excuse stopping you from reaching the unreachable.

Glen Berteau
Senior Pastor, The House Modesto

I would recommend this book first to Christian business people and everyone who would like to impact the world through giving by faith in the name of Jesus. Supernatural giving by faith when God tells you to give before you have the money. In 2 years Ben funded in Mexico 12 churches and completed the majority of 36,000 square foot worship center at the orphanage, *Rancho De Sus Niños*, Tijuana, Mexico. This book will lead you into a giving journey of faith with God that will touch souls for salvation in Christ.

Rev. Steve Horner
Founder, *Rancho De Sus Niños* Orphanage

There are those who tell you how it's done and then there are those who quietly show you how it's done. Ben is the latter. His faith will inspire and challenge you to believe God for the impossible. Ben really is a voice crying in the wilderness, preparing the way of the Lord. He hears the voice of the Lord and is unashamed to share it. His unconventional style brings a freshness that breaks through the noise of the day and points you to Jesus.

If you are ready for inspiring, faith-lifting stories, you will want to read this book.

Gary Heiney
Founder of Samuel's House, Caracas, Venezuela

Ben's relentless pursuit to honor God in seeking to save lost souls in spite of unknown and opposing circumstances challenges us to live the Christian life out loud. He often promised financial support when he had nothing to rely on but trust that God would provide. Journey with him through thousands of miles of darkness, storms, and raging waters, all to provide a better life for those who have need. Ben gives a whole new meaning to "God loves a hilarious giver" (2 Cor. 9:7).

Allen Fisher
World Arm Wrestling Champion

Contents

Introduction • That Dog Won't Hunt

Initially, dogs were bred to hunt. Over time people manipulated the breeding process to produce cute, fluffy canine pets that no longer have the innate desire to hunt. Don't get me wrong—there's nothing wrong with a cuddly pet. But their purpose in life is completely different from the original intent of canine breeders.

I hope you'll excuse the comparison, but some Christians resemble those fluffy dogs. They sit in church, groomed and pretty, but they're unable or unwilling to fulfill the intent for which they were initially created—to hunt. Jesus gave His followers an assignment: to hunt out, or seek, those who are lost. The task is not an easy one. When you follow His commission, trouble will soon follow.

Fluffy dogs cannot hunt. It's not in their nature, their breeding. Other dogs can hunt, but choose not to. I've never been a fluffy dog. In fact, I've been a bad dog who could hunt, but refused. When you think about it, one dog is no different from the other.

The result is the same. Neither honors God with their actions or their life.

A life spent never hunting might be fine for dogs, but is that any place for a person to live? God extends His hand down to change how we live, but we have to reach up and grasp it. We have to want to change. We have to be fully committed. Otherwise, when the heat is on we'll abandon the hunt and run home with our tails tucked between our legs.

I've called this book *Faith without Honor.* As Christians we profess faith in God and His Son. But do we honor Him in our daily lives? Faith without honor is empty faith, a faith that brings God no honor. It's belief without action. That's a sobering thought for any Christian.

It doesn't have to be that way. That is not the life your Creator intended you to live.

> *He renews my strength. He guides me along right paths, bringing honor to his name.* (Psalm 23:3, NLT)

Are you content to sit around doing nothing while others advance the Kingdom of God? If not, this book was written for you. All the stories told in these pages have a common theme: the author did nothing to affect the ending. He merely made the decision to trust God to begin the story. God said in His Word what He is willing to do for those who trust Him. This book is written in the hopes that my message will spark a fire in your heart to stand up and be counted for God.

Faith with honor is described clearly in Psalm 50:15. There are three moving parts:

1) Trust Me in your times of trouble
2) and I will rescue you
3) and you will give Me glory

You've heard the saying "easier said than done"? How true that saying is when applied to the three moving parts! It's never easy to face fear. Everyone wants to bypass the first and second steps and jump directly to the third. That's completely understandable. Who wants to be in trouble or in need of rescue if it can be avoided? The first two parts of this simple equation can make for a hairy ride, and our natural instinct is to avoid difficult circumstances. But the third part, bringing glory to God, doesn't come without the first two.

Most people's troubles start with money. They place their faith in having enough money to bring them fulfillment and deliver them from their troubles. They are afraid to give money to God because they fear the giving might result in having to go without something they want or even need. In other words, they say they have faith in God, but does that faith honor God? No. Their actions honor their god, which is money. They protect and preserve their god by the decisions they make and the things they do.

Christian churches today are filled with different kinds of people. They come from different places and backgrounds, they work at different jobs and pay scales, live in different houses, drive different cars and wear different clothes. But when it comes to trusting and honoring God, they fall into two categories: those who tithe and give offerings to God, and those who don't.

Don't misunderstand: I believe everyone who

loves God wants to give, and to be used by God. But they hold back because of two mighty forces: doubt and fear. Why would any power or principality want to keep you from giving to God? The reason is simple. If you can be kept from trusting God by giving your tithes and offerings, you can be kept from honoring God. God's enemies don't want to see Him honored any more than your enemies want to see you honored.

When you fail to honor God with faith in Him, the plan for your life is stopped because He can't reward those who don't have faith in Him. The blessings God has for you and your family can be stopped, and your destiny can be taken away. It is my hope that this book will encourage you to believe in God's faithfulness, and that you will recover the life you were intended to live.

There is a life of power waiting for you, a higher road to travel on. The map to that highway is often just a different perspective away. Many times in the Bible Jesus didn't change the person or the circumstances they were in. He changed how they saw the circumstances around them. Jesus knew if He could change the way people looked at things, He could transform what they understood and believed. When that happened, their actions would change as well.

People who tithe make up less than ten percent of churchgoers, and they do ninety percent of the work. Most of them are battle tested and true. They have not lived life as observers, but participants. They have learned to trust God. When fear or doubt raises its ugly head, they cut it off with the power of God's Word and His promises to them. These people are not comfortable sitting around getting brushed and groomed every Sunday. They want to go out and hunt. They don't always say the right things and they make some fluffy dogs nervous, but their actions speak louder than words. Nice sounding words without action are a threat to no one. They accomplish nothing except to mislead others into a powerless life of sound bytes.

> *Now someone may argue, "Some people have faith; others have good deeds." But I say, "How can you show me your faith if you don't have good deeds? I will show you my faith by my good deeds." You say you have faith, for you believe that there is one God. Good for you! Even the demons believe this, and they tremble in terror. How foolish! Can't you see that faith without good deeds is useless?* (James 2:18-20, NLT)

In the Old Testament book of Isaiah, chapter seven tells the story of King Ahaz, who faced two powerful armies. The Prophet Isaiah told the king he could ask for a sign from God to prove that God was with him. Ahaz answered with some pretty words: "I wouldn't test the Lord like that!" What a virtuous-sounding reply. It would certainly pass for a righteous statement in most circles today. But they were deceptive words, meant to hide his heart of mistrust in God. His refusal to ask for a test didn't fool Isaiah or God. Ahaz wanted to trust in his money (see 2nd Kings 16:8). He wanted to buy a great army. In other words, he had more faith in what his money could do for him than in what God could do. With his words Ahaz wanted to make it sound and look like he trusted God, but his actions proved otherwise.

There is a monumental truth at work in the life of someone who chooses to have faith in God: if a person can trust God with money, they can trust God with everything. Because money is at the base of most everything, you either rule over it or it rules over you. If you have no faith to tithe and give offerings to God, you have little faith for anything else. A lot of your problems will go away when you begin to trust God with your money.

The faith you have and the fate you have are tied to each other. One follows the other.

Some folks with lots of education, experience, training and capital do nothing with what they've been given. Others, with nothing but faith, have changed the world and brought great honor to God.

It is impossible to get from earth to heaven by performing good deeds, or by tithing and giving offerings. But by doing those things, it is possible to bring some of heaven to earth.

For it is by grace you have been saved, through faith—and this is not from yourselves, it is the gift of God—not by works, so that no one can boast. For we are God's handiwork, created in Christ Jesus to do good works, which God prepared in advance for us to do. (Ephesians 2:8-10, NIV)

Faith begins with believing God can be trusted. No person would have a problem trusting God with their money if God returned what they gave thirty-, sixty- and a hundredfold by the following Friday. If the returns on what you gave came every Friday like clockwork there would be lines outside every Church a mile long with people eager to give every dollar they had or could borrow. The problem with a guaranteed return on Friday is that it would require no faith in God to give it, and God requires faith from anyone who wants to please Him.

> *And it is impossible to please God without faith. Anyone who wants to come to him must believe that God exists and that he rewards those who sincerely seek him.* (Hebrews 11:6, NLT)

For some, the problem with giving to God has nothing to do with believing in Him. Many believe, but still don't give. Instead, they don't trust God's timetable and His plan. If you knew everything God was prepared to do for you when you trusted Him, maybe the faith wouldn't come so hard. The long, restless nights of problems with no solutions would go away.

I've written this book to encourage you, to share with you the things I've seen God do for me, and what I know He will do for you. God is no respecter of persons and what He has done for one He will do for another.

> *Then Peter began to speak: "I now realize how true it is that God does not show favoritism. (Acts 10:34, NIV)*

I realize you hear many stories about giving, from many different sources. Most come from someone who wants something from you. My experiences in this book are told to encourage you to honor God by trusting Him. How and where you do that has nothing to do with me. You can stop living a life of dishonoring God anytime you want. Stop looking for the right words to say and start looking for the right things to do.

When you reach out to God and begin trusting Him with your money, things will start to change immediately. It's one of the great things about giving. It is immediate. The wheels of your future and fortune start turning in your favor at the same moment the money leaves your hand. Suddenly you don't have to hope for things to be better down the road, you know they will. It's like standing next to two gardens, one with seeds you planted and one without. You feel tremendous optimism and hope for the future while gazing at the garden with seeds in the ground. When you glance at the barren ground with nothing planted, what happens? The feelings evaporate.

I've had heartache and troubles caused by my own mistakes and sin, and I am continually learning of God's love as He mercifully brings me into conformity to His vision for my life. I've learned the hard way that, "Good giving does not excuse bad living." On the other hand, I see people every day living their lives without power or direction who have never learned that, "Good living does not excuse bad giving."

Most people try to do what's right, but it seems the human condition always leaves us with something to apologize for. Spending your time and energy regretting the past and trying to change it is a worthless exercise. What's done is done, and your past is in God's hands. Be content to leave it there and instead focus on what is to come. Make some adjustments moving forward, catch a different perspective on what you're doing and understand that no human is perfect. You don't have to be perfect to honor and please God. Have faith in Him and His love for you. Forget about putting your trust in money or the people who have it. You can't trust both. You have to choose one. Jesus clearly said, "You cannot serve both God and money" (Matthew 6:24, NLT). God doesn't care about who you were; He cares about who you are and who you're going to be.

> *I don't mean to say that I have already achieved these things or that I have already reached perfection. But I press on to possess that perfection for which Christ Jesus first possessed me. No, dear brothers and sisters, I have not achieved it, but I focus on this one thing: Forgetting the past and looking forward to what lies ahead, I press on to reach the end of the race and receive the heavenly prize for which God, through Christ Jesus, is calling us.* (Philippians 3:12-14, NLT)

1 • Starting Out

Words are a starting point, necessary and powerful. The most powerful words in the universe are spoken to God when we accept His Son, Jesus, as Master, Redeemer and Lord. These words grant eternal life and move a mortal being from death to life forever. Yet words alone don't prove a person's faith. Without the act of opening your heart and believing, the words alone don't have the power to grant one minute of eternal life. Only God can see and judge an open heart, but any man can apply the smell test to someone's life. Take a big whiff and you'll know immediately if the fish they're peddling is fresh. Every living creature on earth stinks when it's dead. With no proof of action there is no proof of life.

> *"A good tree can't produce bad fruit, and a bad tree can't produce good fruit. A tree is identified by its fruit. Figs are never gathered from thorn bushes, and grapes are not picked from bramble bushes."* (Luke 6:43-44, NLT)

In Numbers 22 we read the story of Balaam the

Sorcerer. An evil king hired him to curse the Israelites. Instead, God used him to bless the Israelites and foretell the coming of the Messiah who would bless the whole world. Even though Balaam was a sorcerer, he believed what God said. Because of that belief God was able to use him. This was a guy who had a conversation with a donkey. Most people would have freaked out if a donkey spoke, but when he was challenged by the donkey Balaam engaged in a normal conversation with it, like he was talking to his cousin.

> *Then the Lord opened the donkey's mouth, and it said to Balaam, "What have I done to you to make you beat me these three times?" Balaam answered the donkey, "You have made a fool of me! If only I had a sword in my hand, I would kill you right now." The donkey said to Balaam, "Am I not your own donkey, which you have always ridden, to this day? Have I been in the habit of doing this to you?" "No," he said.* (Numbers 22:28-31, NIV)

Balaam wasn't a good guy. He later died by the sword because he chose money, sex and power over serving God. Nevertheless, he was not afraid of the king or anyone else. Even though he was a sorcerer, he was fearless and he was used by God. How much more can God use a born-again Christian if they will conquer their fear and believe what God says?

Sometimes the act of speaking the words God gives us requires faith. Most often, though, believing in God and trusting Him involves doing something *after* speaking the words. A person proves what they believe by what they do. Talking proves nothing unless the words are followed by action. A bully intimidates others with tough words only so long. At some point someone is going to punch him in the mouth, and then he has to prove his tough-guy words.

Many people have been sold a bill of goods by a philosophy of words with no follow-up action. They believe words alone will make their life better and bring them closer to God. It's an easy deception to fall into. Who wouldn't want to have every need provided without lifting a finger? That's an easy sell to an easy road that doesn't exist.

Most actions of faith that prove trust at some level are frightening. The simple truth is that faith does not exist in a vacuum without fear. Without the presence of fear there can be no faith. This is true whether you're asking a girl on a date or making a decision that may risk your life. (Sometimes it might be both, depending on what girl you're asking!)

Fear is never comfortable. The concept of receiving blessings without stress, fear or work—using only words—seems like a much better deal. There's only one problem: it doesn't work. Not only that, it leaves you empty with no accomplishments and no honor to God. Faith only exists when someone steps over fear and continues moving forward with action.

Consider this simple illustration. Take a board that is one foot wide, one foot thick and twenty feet long. Lay it on the ground in the parking lot. Start at one end and walk across the board to the other end. Easy, right? Place that same board between two ninety-story buildings a thousand feet in the air. Now walk across the same board from one end to the other. Which walk requires faith? In both cases you are doing exactly the same thing, walking the same distance on the same board. Why does one walk take faith and the other none? The walk across the board a thousand feet in the air has the presence of fear because of the possibility of death. The walk across the parking lot has no consequence at all.

Faith is overcoming the feelings of fear by casting your eyes to heaven. Most fear is based on what *might* happen. It is the threat of what someone predicts, or the circumstances you imagine for yourself if you step out. Like walking across the board a thousand feet in the air, you're afraid of falling before you even take the first step. Fear is the enabler for faith to exist. The next time God moves you into a position that scares you, don't pray for an unlocked door as you are running out of the room. Instead, ask for courage to stand and fight in faith to accomplish the task He has set before you. Your destiny is at stake, and so is the honor that belongs to God when He rescues you. Make it count.

It is only through faith in God's Word and His ability to rescue and deliver you that you will discover His plan for your life. Fear of being put in a position to require God's deliverance will keep you from honoring God for that rescue, and keep you from living a life of purpose and destiny.

God will not give you a life that makes Him unnecessary so that you can worship Him at your leisure. If you have a life like that, it's a life you've given to yourself.

As discussed in the introduction, there are three moving parts to bringing God honor. The first part is trouble. The second part is rescue. And third is honoring God.

Then call on me when you are in trouble, and I will rescue you, and you will give me glory. (Psalm 50:15, NLT)

Remove the first part and there is no second or third part. Remove the trouble and there is no rescue or glory. So why do so many people look for a way to remove trouble from their lives?

Because needing a rescue isn't fun. We'll do whatever we can to avoid it. You can spend time and money driving around and buying books and tapes and going to seminars and churches until you die, but where is the honor in that? God is not honored by a person who stands behind words, but doesn't follow through with action. When you move forward to do more than just talk, trouble will be waiting for you. But so will the rescue. And so will the honor.

There are two sides to the cross, the front side and the back side. On the front side the disciples cowered in fear looking for answers in the natural world to deliver or rescue them from trouble. On the back side of the cross the same men faced danger and obstacles, expecting miracles by the power of Jesus Christ to rescue them.

On the front side of the cross the disciples screamed in terror when the boat was sinking (Mark 4:38). They asked Jesus if he cared that they perished. When Jesus was arrested and crucified, they were nowhere to be found.

On the back side of the cross, the disciples were threatened by the council (Acts 4:18), and put in prison to await an uncertain future (Acts 5:18). Those same terrified men no longer cried out to God in fear for their lives, but called the circumstances a "threat" (Acts 5:29). The disciples didn't ask to be saved. They asked for power and miracles in the name of Jesus.

Fear is always tied to some kind of threat of what the devil or someone says they will do to you. The only thing someone can do against God's plan for your life is threaten, because they don't have the power to do anything else. If a threat comes against God and His plan for your life, it is absolutely meaningless. It may look and sound intimidating, but see it for what it is: just another giant looking to lose his head.

Anyone who knows Christ as their King has gone to the back side of the cross when they accepted Him and His power. The problem is that time and circumstance can drag us back to the front side of the cross, where we find ourselves living in fear again. We worry about what's going to happen to us. If you dread the future, the life of those fluffy dogs in the pews starts to look pretty good. That's when you open the Book and see what Jesus has to say about your circumstance. Get back around to the other side of the cross where you belong. Sure, dogs that hunt need a rescue every now and again, but the honor and glory they bring back to their Master is well worth it.

Jesus showed people how to see things differently for one purpose: to enable them to do things differently. He told stories and asked questions in order to change people's perspective and therefore to enable them to change what they did. In a story about a man robbed and left in a ditch, He asked His listeners, "Who was the neighbor to this man?" That story changed how people looked at Samaritans. He intervened when an angry crowd of men were ready to kill a woman for her sin, and challenged them to throw the stones if they had no sin themselves. His actions caused each man to quietly walk away. In both cases Jesus altered how people looked at others, and it changed what they thought and what they did. If you ask Him, Jesus can change how you see a challenge and the fear that comes from moving into the unknown. Let the Holy Spirit take you through His Word and show you the things Jesus wants you to see so you can honor Him by your actions, proving His power. The power of words is never proved without application.

God wants to build our faith so we can make a difference in the world for Him. He desires to demonstrate that bringing Him honor through faith in action can overcome any lack of talent or backing. The Bible is full of stories of ordinary people who chose to trust God alone and rely only on His backing. These folks were wildly successful because God is powerful. There are also stories of people who chose honor for themselves. They trusted in their own riches and power, and they met disaster. Both these groups of people wanted to succeed, and they each had their own perspective of how to accomplish that success. The Bible demonstrates that one method works and the other doesn't.

The person who does nothing in faith and brings no honor to God will bore you to death with stories of what someone else did. People who move in faith say very little. Their actions speak for them. Like pulling the pin on a hand grenade, the silence is followed by a bang.

Jesus asked questions and made statements about money, fame, sex and power. He wanted to change how people viewed the trophy collections of successful men. In changing how they viewed these things, He could get them to change the decisions they made.

What good is it for someone to gain the whole world, yet forfeit their soul? (Mark 8:36, NIV)

God still speaks to man. His Word is relevant to our lives if we will let it be relevant without endless analysis and excuses while sitting around doing nothing. Jesus will speak to you if you listen for the voice of His Spirit. His words need not be audible to be heard. They will echo in your soul and bring iron to your spine as you turn the pages of His Book and realize that He has a plan for your life to bring Him honor. God loves you. Do you think His plan for these end times doesn't include you? Of course it does! Let Him change your perception of the need that presents itself to you and be a part of what God is doing as a participant and not as an observer. Take the bull by the horns and wrestle that thing down. Don't let someone else take the blessing that was meant for you! Whether it's your pastor describing a new building that has to be purchased, a missionary who needs help funding a school or someone who just needs a hand up who has fallen next to you, get involved and make a commitment to do more than you can with the resources you have. By doing this you are depending on God and His resources and you're putting yourself in the wheelhouse of His power! You'll be sorry forever if you lose the opportunity. It won't come your way again because God will not deny the petition of those in need who trust and love Him. He will just use someone else to answer their prayers and you'll be put in the fluffy dog pew of observers whether you want to be there or not. Spectators bring glory and honor to no one, only players and participants are allowed to do that. What kind of sound do you want ringing out when you cast your crowns at Jesus's feet? How will He be honored by what you have done? Trust and honor God with your actions and take your rightful place in the field of battle. There is no other place that will satisfy your soul.

Jesus is coming soon to gather us home. He died for a million and He died for the one. He has strategically placed you in a position to make a difference, but it will all be for nothing if you do nothing.

2 • Beginning of Faith to Give

When I started working as a boy, I always gave ten percent of my earnings to the Church. It wasn't hard because there were no other options; it's what we were taught to do. I milked cows and worked for dollars here and there. When I got my car at sixteen I got a gardening job taking care of the rich people's houses. I worked from dawn until school started, and then after school I had a job pumping gas at the local Gulf gas station till ten o'clock at night. Minimum wage was $1.65 an hour and I was making $2.10, so I was walking in tall cotton in those days. By the time I was a senior, I found work as a carpenter, driving dump trucks and skinning cats. (Cat skinning means that I operated caterpillar bulldozers pushing rock at a quarry.) I was earning more money than most of my teachers, and thought I had life figured out. What 18-year-old doesn't?

Money was never a problem for me. Most of the time I had a pocketful and I always made sure to give ten percent to Ma to take down to the church house. Every time I'd hand her my tithe money she would say, "Honey why don't you come down to church with me on Sunday and give it to the Lord yourself?" I wasn't serving God and I didn't want to give Him a bad name by having me at His place, so I didn't hang around there much. I knew that God loved me and I can't remember from my earliest day not loving Him, but I figured He understood that I couldn't go down to that church house and listen to somebody talk about what God did 2,000 years ago, while they sat around doing nothing now.

I was raised in a church that taught once you were saved you were always saved. As long as I wasn't going to hell for the things I was doing, the rest of it didn't matter to me. Whether or not that is right or wrong I don't know, but one thing is for sure: thinking I was hell-proof sent me on a long road filled with heartbreak and pain.

I didn't know how God always managed to take care of me, I just knew He did. I had a lunch box theology that put God as the head of a big factory. I was like a kid walking to school with his lunchbox past the giant factory building owned by my dad, smokestacks reaching into the sky. I was never sure what my dad did up in the boardroom of that factory, but I knew he was good at it so he wouldn't have a problem packing a good lunch into my lunchbox for school that day. What was there to worry about?

I remember the first time I ever hesitated in giving God back His share of my paycheck. It happened one morning while I was sitting at the kitchen table, staring at my checkbook. I was 18. I had fifty bucks left in my checking account and forty of it belonged to God. I had only made $400 that month because of the recession and gas shortage, and after I paid my bills fifty bucks was all that was left over. I hadn't been out of high school long, and the rock quarry where I was working had shut down for the winter. The economy was in the tank and building projects were all but nonexistent. I had managed to score a full tank of gas and was looking forward to a fun weekend skiing in Tahoe with my pals. I knew if I wrote a check to Ma for God's cut I wouldn't be skiing that weekend. Fifty bucks would barely cover the cost of the trip as it was. It was the first time I remember contemplating taking part of God's share of my income. I started with some of the same thoughts and justifications that most people who steal probably use today. Thoughts like, "I'll only take some of it," or "I'll pay it back later," or "I need it more than He does right now," or "He won't miss it anyway."

I sat at that kitchen table for what seemed like an hour performing mental gymnastics to justify doing what I already knew was wrong. God had always taken care of me and what kind of man would I be now to steal from Him when times got rough?

Finally I decided that I just couldn't walk across that crooked bridge and bite the hand that had always fed me. I wrote a check to the church and handed it to Ma, and then I called my buddies and told them I wasn't going skiing. About five seconds after I hung the phone up somebody knocked at the front door. We didn't get many visitors to the ranch out in Schellville, California. We lived miles from town and no one ventured out to those parts unless they had business.

Ma went to the door and a few moments later she called, "Benny there is someone at the door for you."

I walked the short distance from one room to the other in the old farmhouse. I recognized the big man standing at the door as the owner of the largest road construction company in town. We said our hellos while I shook his monster hand, and then he said, "Ben, I know you're a good cat skinner and truck driver, and I could use you help if you're looking for work." He explained that his company had been given a large county contract to build miles of road, and if I was ready I could go to work that day.

My new boss asked if I wanted to follow him out to the yard and I quickly said, "Yeah!"

"Alright then, let's go."

He turned toward his truck with a smile of amusement at my enthusiasm. As I opened the door to my car I felt a Presence that caused my heart to melt. Soon the taste of salty tears made its way to my mouth. Suddenly I was in the presence of a loving God. I knew He was there and I knew He was mindful of me, and that I could trust Him to take care of me. I did not dishonor Him by stealing from Him. I honored Him for what He had always done for me, and He did not disappoint me.

> *Once I was young, and now I am old. Yet I have never seen the godly abandoned or their children begging for bread.* (Psalm 37:25, NLT)

I went to work that day driving a Peterbilt bottom dump truck an hour after I hung the phone up from my buddies who were on their way to the mountains to go skiing. I worked through the whole winter making six bucks an hour when there was no work to be found anywhere. Not only that, but I found plenty of days to go skiing that year, and I never worried about being able to afford to go.

Most of us have heard the term, "blind faith." I think that's where most Christians begin with tithing, or giving to God. It's blind faith because they have never offered a tenth of what they make to God and then watched God alter the course of their life with blessings. They have no basis to believe other than what they've read or heard. Once they have experienced living in the supernatural realm of divine financial blessing, their faith can begin to grow. They have a well of proof from which to draw. It's a lifelong exercise, and perfect faith is never attained because God will keep drawing you in deeper and deeper, in order to make your faith stronger and stronger. Just when you think you have conquered the fear of spending one amount, the Lord will bring a greater need that will require more faith and a larger amount. Each time this happens, you can draw from your past experience with God's provisions and move forward again into the unknown.

The things I believe to be true about God are based ten percent on what I have read and ninety percent on what I have lived. This is a tremendous advantage when stepping into the unknown, but it wasn't always so. Each person is given a measure of faith to begin with, and it is up to them to choose to believe what they have read or what they are told. The only real evidence of their belief is measured by their actions. As they move on what they say they believe, their faith becomes based on what they *know* and not just what they hope is true. People whose beliefs are ninety percent based on what they have read and ten percent on what they have lived have very little confidence in an unproven God. They bring God little honor or glory for what He has not done in their lives.

When the Israelite army faced Goliath, a million men stood shivering in their boots, deathly afraid. They were so afraid that even King Saul's promise of paying no taxes, marrying his daughter, and moving into the palace was enough to overcome their fear. You'd think there would be at least one really awful-looking man who'd jump at the chance in order to marry a beautiful princess. When most of your faith comes from what you've heard and not what you've done, there's not much to draw from when you need faith to step out. Confidence is hard to find when you look around and see only people who are good talkers, but who are just as chicken as you.

David knew God's Word but he also knew what it was like to *live* God's Word and watch God's power move around and through him. This was an advantage he held over all the men in the army, and he used it to move past fear and find his destiny. He drew from his experience trusting God for victory over the lion and the bear, and he found the faith he needed to fight Goliath. In doing so he brought honor and glory to his God. David didn't draw his courage from what he read, he got it from what he had lived!

But David said to Saul, "Your servant has been keeping his father's sheep. When a lion or a bear came and carried off a sheep from the flock, I went after it, struck it and rescued the sheep from its mouth. When it turned on me, I seized it by its hair, struck it and killed it. Your servant has killed both the lion and the bear; this uncircumcised

Philistine will be like one of them, because he has defied the armies of the living God. (1 Samuel 17:34-36, NIV)

How can you draw courage from something you never did? It's like trying to draw water from an empty well. At some point your destiny will become clear and the challenge will require you to conquer fear before moving forward. If you have nothing to draw from you won't be successful. The truth is most people won't even try. David had to fight Goliath because Goliath was his provision from God to be the king instead of a farmer. The day is coming when you will have to face the same challenge. His name may not be Goliath, but the obstacle standing in your way will be just as scary. If your faith is not based on past experience with God's provision, you will not answer the challenge and you will not find your destiny. The honor and glory to God that would have come from your faith in Him will never arrive at His Throne. Like your words without action, there will only be an empty space void of accomplishment in place of a crown. Don't give away the everlasting honor you can bring God because of selfishness or fear in a temporary world.

The provision for your destiny will always come in the form of a problem you can't solve without His help. Receiving His help will always be based on faith in Him. Most of the stories in the Bible are of people with destiny and problems. Those who trusted God conquered the problem and fulfilled their destiny. Even Jesus had a problem in front of His destiny; it was called the cross. He conquered the cross and fulfilled His destiny to become the Savior of the world.

Every person has to start somewhere. Today is as good as any other day to start building a life experience of faith so you don't end up holding a bag of air when the heat is on. The first and easiest step to take is to stop trusting money and start trusting God. I say it's easy because writing a check takes no effort or physical strength, but it's not so easy if you love money.

Regardless of whether you find giving hard or easy, if you can't get past the first step, you're done. Recognize that everything you have belongs to God, and He has instructed you to return a portion to Him. It's a sowing-and-reaping formula the Creator designed so you can be blessed and cared for financially. He hasn't come up with any new formulas since He made the planet that will work, regardless what your accountant may think. God won't allow anyone to reach their destiny or bring Him honor that is ripping Him off. When you trust God with a tenth of your money, you can begin to trust Him with everything else because money will lose its power over you. Money will no longer govern how you make decisions. When the Holy Spirit tells you to move, you can move without being paralyzed by indecision and fear.

Jesus does not want to come back for His children when there are the fewest children to be taken. He does not want to leave any behind. His goal isn't to wait until there is an absolute bare minimum of believers and then pop down and hammer everyone who doesn't believe. Jesus wants to have His apron full when He comes to take His followers home. I know plenty of people who have dedicated their life to the pursuit of bringing souls into the kingdom, but there's a dire shortage of working folks who are willing to trust God with their money so these dedicated Gospel workers have the funds to go.

I believe the current situation is about to change. I believe people are getting hungry enough for God and His destiny for their life that they are no longer willing to let others foot the bill for missions work while they squirrel away a few extra dollars to live an unsatisfied life. People are going to start stepping out to pursue their life and destiny in God, because they know the time is getting short. There will not be another opportunity down the road. The only reason God hasn't sent Jesus down here yet is He wants more people to make it to heaven, and in order for that to happen they need to believe and repent.

The Lord isn't really being slow about his promise, as some people think. No, he is being patient for your sake. He does not want anyone to be destroyed, but wants everyone to repent. (2 Peter 3:9, NLT)

Reaching souls cost money, and God is preparing to shower blessings on people who will trust Him with what they have so He can give them much more. If He can trust you with a little, He can trust you with a lot and it's going to take a lot to finance this last great revival before the coming of the Lord.

His master replied, 'Well done, good and faithful servant! You have been faithful with a few things; I will put you in charge of many things. Come and share your master's happiness! (Matthew 25:21, NIV)

Starting a conversation about giving money and

finding your destiny makes a lot of people nervous. They start looking for the door. It's kind of like discussing the pain of the last rep when driving iron in the gym. The subject doesn't interest anyone who is happy lifting ninety pounds, but those who desire something more will listen and pursue it.

You can't talk to someone who has no passion for the lost about serving God. They don't understand how anyone could have a passion for such a thing. It's like trying to talk about art to someone who loves dragsters. Most dragster guys won't listen because they don't want to hear about nineteenth century impressionism. They want to hear about burning rubber. The same thing applies when trying to talk about dragsters to most art buffs. The art buff may politely listen but he's not hearing a word you say until the conversation turns to Monet or Michelangelo.

Those who have the Holy Spirit in them are driven to bring the lost into the kingdom for Christ, and that's what they want to talk about. When most people are saved it's the first thing they want to do, but time and fear quench the fire of the Holy Spirit. They settle for a faith without risk. Their faith brings no honor to God because they won't let God put them into a position—whether emotional, physical or financial—that only God can deliver them from. A day is coming that no believer should want to miss, but many will. It's the day when all those who followed Jesus with their actions and not just their words will meet. They will come from the halls of time and gather together in heaven at a party unlike any other since time began. Many Christians who today don't want to trust God, fight for Jesus, and honor Him with their actions will wish they had fought for Him then.

I remember a time in high school when we had just finished a hard fought football game against a rival town. Some of the guys on the opposing team had a lot to say after the game. A couple of us went over to have a word with the players. One of the big linebackers from their team suggested we talk about our opinions out behind the bleachers after we got our gear off. We thought that was a great idea.

About an hour later we met in the dark field behind the bleachers and stood face to face. There were about ten or fifteen guys up front and twenty in the back from each town. It was a cold December night, and our breath created clouds of steam. Hearts pounded in the chests of fifty guys ready to mix it up. The size of the fighters didn't matter; there were big guys and little guys on both sides, and most of the big guys ran when the blood flowed anyway. The bigger guys were used to bullying their way through life and backing people down with the sheer intimidation of their size alone. Most didn't know how to throw a punch and make it count. They were just propped up in the front to scare the weaker ones. But the guys who had been around knew they were merely cardboard heroes, and our eyes scanned the line to spot the real fighters.

When the first fist flew and the sound of a landed punch cracked out into the night air, the fight was on. Within seconds most of the front line and all of the back line were gone. They sprinted away on both sides, scrambling for their lives. I was on the ground on top of some guy and caught a boot to the head that sent me rolling. When I made it to my feet all I could see of the crowd that had been standing there seconds before were the back pockets of their 501 jeans and their elbows.

Only four or five of us stood and fought, and the rest disappeared into the night like a mirage. We did our best and gave better than we got until the cops showed up. The five of us hopped over the fence and made our way through the back streets of town. My buddy Eddy was having a party that night. We snuck out to Eddy's barn in the back, not knowing who might be in the driveway and cleaned ourselves up at the trough. There wasn't much we could do with our ripped-up clothes, so Eddy went inside and brought us out some shirts and a coat or two. When we eventually joined the party, you could pick out the fighters by the cuts and bruises on their hands and faces, and the limp they carried when they walked, not to mention the funky clothes we wore that Eddy gave us that didn't fit. The five of us gathered in the kitchen with crooked and swollen smiles, laughing as we reveled in the battle from a few hours earlier. Dozens of kids at the party that night wanted to join us in Eddy's kitchen to recount the battle, but they couldn't. They'd deserted the fight, and regretted it. When it came their time to step up, they were just too scared. Now that it was over and we were all reasonably okay, they wished they'd had the courage to take part. Those who didn't fight were defeated that night and they never threw a punch, never got hit. Victory was theirs for the taking and they accepted defeat, not because they couldn't win but because they were afraid to try.

Fear will take everything God has for your future away from you. Don't let it. Honor is gained from overcoming fear. Nothing is gained by letting fear overcome you. If Jesus deserves honor, shouldn't we go out and get Him some?

Decisions are easy after-the-fact, in the comfort of a warm light kitchen. Very few want to make the same decision on a dark wet field when the outcome is uncertain. The merits of what went down that night, right or wrong, are not being offered for debate. Pride fuels most violence and young men are destroyed by wrong decisions based on their own insecurities. We were spared that night from someone getting really hurt and ruining someone's life and I'm not an advocate of guys participating in fist fights to feed egos. The point isn't to glorify fists and the fight, it's to point out the fear and circumstances surrounding the fight and the guys who chose to run after making a verbal commitment.

Don't make a commitment to fight for the cause of Christ and then run at the first sign of trouble. Sharing the Gospel and furthering the kingdom of God is not always a neat and tidy affair. Sometimes things can get messy. Circumstances change, some people go away, and others disappoint or hurt you. The stress of feeling like you're standing alone with no escape in sight can rattle the strongest Christian. It rattled Elijah (1 Kings 19) and it will rattle you, but God doesn't get rattled. He will bring you through and He will accomplish His plan for your life if you will trust and follow Him. One of the patches we wear when we ride says, "Let the dead bury the dead" (Matthew 8:22). Everybody can find an excuse when Jesus says, "Let's go," but if you do, you're out. There's no rattles to overcome if you excuse your way out, but there's no glory or honor to God if you do.

One thing is certain: there is no honor in running

away in fear from a fight that you showed up for. If you don't want to fight, then stay home. Don't tell God that you're ready to serve Him while in the warm fuzzy church pew of the fluffy dogs, and then back down when the Lord brings you over to sit in the pews with the hunting dogs and up to the line to make a difference for Him. Your victory brings Him honor, and He sent His Son Jesus to guarantee that victory. The battle is the Lord's. At a bare minimum, you need to show up and not run away.

If you think a blow dealt by the enemy in a spiritual battle hurts less than a left hook to the jaw in a physical battle, you'd be wrong. Trusting God and engaging the enemy to save souls is every bit as frightening as any physical fight. You either cross over and go, or you don't. You punch or run. There is no middle ground.

Would you rather have a tooth knocked out, or lose $10 million? I don't know anybody who wouldn't rather lose a tooth, given the choice. Which one is more dreadful and scary? Not having money or losing money frightens a lot of people. That's the reason so many people don't honor God with their giving. It scares them.

Jesus is the Lion and the Lamb. He was the most courageous Man who ever lived. He never backed off from anybody unless He had a reason, and the reason was never fear. When He returns as a Lion, a lot of people will be disappointed. They are expecting the Lamb to sit and take another beating. (Read your Bible.) You need both the Lion and the Lamb to succeed at the task the Lord is giving you, and you will not fail moving forward if you purpose in heart to trust God and have faith that honors Him.

And from the days of John the Baptist until now the kingdom of heaven suffers violence, and the violent take it by force. (Matthew 11:12, NKJV)

But one of the twenty-four elders said to me, "Stop weeping! Look, the Lion of the tribe of Judah, the heir to David's throne, has won the victory. He is worthy to open the scroll and its seven seals." (Revelation 5:5, NLT)

When you find the faith and courage to give to God, everything else you need will follow. There is no security in money anyway, it's just an illusion. If you are having a hard time with habits or hang ups, His presence will be near to help you overcome them. When you need direction in business during hard times, He will keep you in the game until it turns around. This is a spiritual fight we are in. Every time you give to God with faith that He will replenish you, it is a blow landed on the chops of the enemy as the resources you supply brings souls into the Kingdom of God.

They will not be disgraced in hard times; even in famine they will have more than enough. (Psalm 37:19, NLT)

There is nothing God won't do for a person who puts His agenda at the top of their priority list. Some of the biggest givers to the Lord I know have some of the coolest stuff. They own and enjoy things, but the things don't ever own them.

Take delight in the Lord, and he will give you your heart's desires. Commit everything you do to the Lord. Trust him, and he will help you. (Psalm 37:4-5, NLT)

Wherever givers find themselves, their profession of faith never changes. Even when they are on the bottom, their attitude is the same because they know they will not be there long. Besides, every time I've been at the bottom I needed to be there for an adjustment, not because God couldn't keep me from being there. As soon as I got my eyes and ears readjusted, back up we went.

You'll never see a tither fretting in the halls of a court room or panicked at the table in a board room, because even there they know God has the final word. Time is always on their side; their God controls the clock and they trust Him with it.

He will make your innocence radiate like the dawn, and the justice of your cause will shine like the noonday sun. (Psalm 37:6, NLT)

What is about to happen on the earth was prophesied by the Prophet Joel more than 2,800 years ago. A Gentile Physician named Luke saw part of it happening 2,000 years ago. Now the rest of us will witness God's finale in these last days. God has an open door of invitation to anyone who will trust Him and be straight with Him. He will allow you to play a part in the greatest battle in history if you let Him.

No, what you see was predicted long ago by the prophet Joel: 'In the last days,' God says, 'I will pour out my Spirit upon all people. Your sons and daughters will prophesy. Your young men will see visions, and your old men will dream dreams. In those days I will pour out my Spirit even on my servants—men and women alike—and they will prophesy.' (Acts 2:16-18, NLT)

In real life situations, if we know that time is short we make decisions differently. A coach might call a play in a football game differently with thirty seconds left on the clock than he would if there were ten minutes. A businessman may decide to buy a piece of equipment on December 31, if he discovers the price will jump $100,000 on January 1. You might leave today on a trip if a big storm is blowing in tomorrow. Time is important to God. He invented time specifically for events here on the earth. There is no time in heaven. Time affects the rate and the intensity of the pursuit. Jesus is coming soon, there is very little time left on the game clock. Strict attention must be paid to what play is being brought onto the field, because it might be the last play. It's like my Dad used to say when our options were running out, "Make it count, son."

As long as it is day, we must do the works of him who sent me. Night is coming, when no one can work. (John 9:4, NIV)

3 • A Trip to Cabo

In my travels, I've discovered that often the problems I encounter aren't really problems at all. They're opportunities to honor God and bless others.

A few years ago I flew my plane to Cabo San Lucas, Mexico to speak at a Missions Conference. My friend Joe came along. We landed in San Diego for fuel and to pick up another buddy, Steve, who was coming across the border from Mexico to meet us. We got a late start and decided to spend the night in San Diego. It's illegal to fly at night in Mexico in a private plane, probably because of the drug transportation problem, and I'd had some run-in's with the Mexican authorities before. I sure didn't want to get caught flying after sunset down there.

By the time we landed in San Diego it was dark and the small flight center on the field was closed. We were making decisions on the move, and I hadn't made any reservations to be picked up or a place to stay. I figured we'd just find a motel somewhere near the border and hole-up for the night. We called a cab and were told it would be about thirty minutes. An hour later the cab driver pulled in, looked at me and Joe, and then drove away! After a moment of surprise, we started laughing, "Can you believe that guy!?" I asked Joe.

I got back on the cell and called the dispatcher, who apologized and said she'd send the driver back. We waited another hour with two more phone calls to the cab company; still no cab.

We had a seat on our duffle bags and waited for another two hours before the cab returned. I had already determined to be nice and accept his apology. When you travel for Jesus, you travel with power and you don't want to do anything to grieve His Spirit and cause His power to leave. If the Holy Spirit leaves, your power and direction goes with Him, and you become bait for whatever fish that wants to take a bite out of you.

Joe and I started to walk toward the cab, but before I could open the door he took off again! I whistled at him and he just kept driving. I looked at Joe and asked, "What the heck is going on?!" Joe shook his head. "The guy must be on dope or something."

It was now late at night and we had been trying to get a ride for the better part of two hours. Joe said, "Should we call another cab company?"

I said, "No, man. We need to forget about the cab and try to figure out what the Holy Spirit has planned for us tonight."

I learned a long time ago that when things happen that should not be happening, or when things don't happen that should, stop. God is adjusting your timeline and you need to get synced up with His schedule of events. I've learned to stop and take a look around before making any further decisions. Many people continue on the same course, and then miss what God has for them to see or do.

If you were walking down the street and turned a corner to see a truck floating 10 feet in the air, you wouldn't just shrug your shoulders and keep walking. You'd stop and check out the surroundings, because what's going on is out of the ordinary. Something happening that should not be happening. The event is something from the supernatural inserting itself into the natural, and it is for a reason.

I told Joe we needed to walk around and see if there was anybody at this old military air base. Brown field is only a couple hundred yards from the Mexican border, and the only lights were those out on the tarmac where our plane was parked. The hangars off in the distance were mostly dark. I noticed a light in a small window in one of the hangars, so we walked over to see if anybody was around. To my surprise the hangar door was open and inside was a real nice gal sitting at a desk. Was she the reason for our delay? We struck up a conversation, but the Spirit didn't give me any indication she was. I still had the feeling that our time and place wasn't synced up yet. I asked if she knew where we could get a car. "I have a car here," she said. "It was for a flight that cancelled tonight. I could let you rent it if you'd like." I had the feeling that we were getting closer to our Holy Ghost timeline because things were starting to click and work out. I told her we would take the car.

As she was filling out the paperwork the cab driver walked into the hangar and announces he's there to pick us up! I had no idea how the driver even found this hangar or how he knew we were in there. I instantly knew the driver was not from the Lord and that we were supposed to stay on the course we were now on. I told the driver to beat it, he was two and half hours late and we had already rented a car. The man put up a big stink over us not taking his cab after he drove all the way out there, and he really tried to get us into his cab, but I sent him packing. (So much for the earlier promise I made to myself to accept his apology.) As it turned out we would have never completed our God-assigned task that night had we been dropped off at a motel by that cab driver.

Joe and I took the rental car and drove east from the airport about fifteen miles and found a little motel. I was keenly aware of all of our surroundings, waiting for the prompting of the Holy Spirit to give us directions. I didn't think the motel was the place we were destined for because the cab driver could have dropped us off there.

I told Joe that I knew we were both tired but we needed to take a drive and let things play out. I figured we go find some coffee and food somewhere and let the evening unfold.

We drove around the desert for thirty minutes looking for some place that was open, and finally found a small café with the lights on. The place was completely empty and no one was at the counter. We slid into a booth in the corner. The waitress treated us the same way as the cab driver. She kept walking around like we weren't even there, and then disappeared for ten minutes. I started to think maybe the café was closed, but the hours of operation listed on the front door said they were open till midnight. After ten or fifteen minutes she finally came over and asked us what we wanted to order. By then I felt uneasy about our location and timeline, so I said we both just wanted a cup of coffee.

When the waitress left Joe wanted to know why we didn't order any food. We were both really hungry. I told him I had the feeling our timing was still off. I thought we might be in the right place, but we were still too early. I suggested we finish our coffee and go to the car and pray, and asked him to go along with me on this for a little while longer. We finished our coffee, went out to the car and asked God what we should do. The only Word we got was to wait. So we waited. Thirty minutes. Forty minutes. Fifty minutes. Finally an hour passed sitting in a tiny rental car in the rain in a barren parking lot in front of an empty restaurant.

I had the windows down to keep them from fogging up and the rain was landing on my shoulder when Joe said, "Hey man, are you sure about this? I'm pretty tired and I'm still really hungry." We both started laughing. I told him, "I'm tired too, Brother, but let's not quit now. We've got a lot of time invested in this excellent adventure. We're only seeing things in part, but the part I see says wait."

Now we see things imperfectly, like puzzling reflections in a mirror, but then we will see everything with perfect clarity. All that I know now is partial and incomplete, but then I will know everything completely, just as God now knows me completely. (1 Corinthians 13:12, NLT)

Another half hour passed before I saw a shadowy figure in the distance heading our way. As it got closer I saw that it was a couple holding hands, coming towards the restaurant behind us. I yelled at

Joe who was half asleep against his door. "That's it, there they are!" Joe leaned forward as I was opening the door and asked, "What's it?" I pointed. "Right there. That's them. Let's go!"

We jumped out of the car and hurried to the front door, arriving as the couple was ready to go into the café. I grabbed the door handle in front of them and then stopped without opening it. I asked, "How are you two pilgrims doing tonight?" They were an older couple who had the look of two people that had been together for a long time. The man answered, "Fine, thanks." Then I said, "I want you to know before we go into this restaurant that the Living God has sent us here for you tonight. You can order whatever you want on the menu and anything else you need to get home is going to be taken care of. Jesus heard your prayers tonight and has sent us to you."

I had no idea who this couple was or what their needs were but I knew they were in trouble and needed to get home as soon as I saw them in the shadows approaching the café. The Holy Spirit doesn't need to use words. He can speak to His servants in many different ways. I have had Him speak to me in words and numbers but also in concepts, visions, dreams, through the Bible, through a brother or sister in the Lord and even through a movie in the theater. When you see a beautiful sunset you don't have to say to yourself that it is beautiful to understand that it is beautiful. Just seeing it is to understand what beauty is. When you see a baby colt just born in the field being cared for by its mother do you have to speak or see the word love to understand what love is? It's a feeling, and words aren't always necessary. One thing is for sure, God will never tell you something that is contrary to what is written in the Bible. If you are wondering why the Master never speaks to you, maybe it's because you aren't serving. Why would a master tell a servant to do anything when he knows the servant won't serve?

The lady fell into her husband's arms and began crying. He just lowered his head into hers. After they calmed down and we got inside to a table they told us their story. They had driven to Mexico from a church in Oregon with supplies for an orphanage. On the return trip home, they were robbed at the border. They lost everything—cash, wallet and cell phone. They had tried to use a pay phone with the little change they had to call for help, but had been unable to contact anyone. They were hungry, scared and alone, praying in their old truck that God would help them. They'd driven as far as they could on the gas they had, and couldn't go any further than the parking lot of this deserted café in the desert where Joe and I were waiting for them in a fogged up rental car. All they had was some change from the ashtray and they were going inside to share a cup of coffee.

We bought them a big dinner with dessert, and I asked the old man what kind of mileage his truck got. He told me around 14 miles per gallon, so I gave him $300 bucks for fuel and food to get home and enough extra to rent a room for the night. Then we were done. We accomplished our mission that night when we didn't even know what our mission was.

The next morning we were wheels up at 7:00 a.m., headed down Mexico way at two hundred miles an hour. We were ready for whatever was coming because we knew that God was already there.

Our stop in San Diego and the hassle of things

not going as we planned wasn't about us. It was about the couple we met in the parking lot. God moved time and space to get us there, to be His answer to that couple's prayer. He answered our prayer too, because we prayed to be used for His Glory and to honor Him on that trip. What seemed like problems to us weren't problems at all; they were blessings. We were blessed by God when He trusted us to take care of a request He received, and He was preparing us for what was to come when we got to Cabo.

Timelines affect the speed in which we perform, and the intensity of the pursuit.

When we got down to the conference, we were still feeling the effects of being in close proximity to the Holy Spirit. I expected a great meeting that night. I had made financial commitments of $600,000 to three different ministries that year, and I made it clear to the missionary running the conference that I couldn't help him financially. I would come and speak, but that was as far as I could commit. My business was running on fumes, and I didn't have any dough to give to him because there was six hundred grand of unpaid pledges in front of him.

That night as I stood on the balcony of the hotel looking at the ocean, I asked the Lord what He would have me say to these people who had come to this conference. They were all gathered around a bonfire at the water's edge below, waiting for the meeting to start at seven o'clock. The missionary who was sponsoring the conference was building Bible schools and churches around the world, and we were right in the middle of a brutal recession unmatched since 1929. Money was scarce and bankers laughed in my face when I asked for a loan. The missionary told me before I agreed to speak that they hoped to raise $50,000 for the work he was doing for the Lord.

As I stood looking down on all these good people who had come from all over the U.S. to hear about and help in God's work, I was humbled at the sacrifice they were willing to make to be there. "Lord," I asked again, "what do You want me to say and do here?" I was looking for a concept or an idea of what He wanted me to do. I didn't have a clue. I was broke so I had nothing to give. I'm not a preacher so I had no sermon to deliver either. I wasn't clear on what I had to contribute to this thing.

My thoughts wandered to the times I had fished these waters with my buddies. Once I'd landed a big marlin. In the theater of my mind, right when I was reeling in that giant fish, the Lord popped a number into my head. $100,000.

I snapped back to reality. Did the Holy Spirit just say that to me? The number made my hands perspire. I said, "Lord, I don't have a $100,000 and I'm still $600,000 behind on the other mission's stuff you told me to do." Then the Lord told me to look at the people down on the beach. As I did He explained to me that a leader has to lead from the boat, and not the shore. He told me that I couldn't shout instructions on how to steer the boat while on dry land and expect people to listen. I needed to be in the boat for people to hear me.

I don't think I have ever been down further financially than in '07 and '08. God told me that I needed to keep trusting Him so I could help others to trust Him too. (That's the reason I wrote this book.) I took a deep breath and said, "Lord, You know I don't have a hundred grand. Unless You move, I'm dead in the water. I may as well tell that guy I'll give him $10,000,000. But I guess it doesn't matter to you what the amount is anyway."

I don't remember exactly what I said that night during my thirty-minute talk, but that's not unusual. I figure the mail being delivered is from God to someone else and not for me. I'm just the postman, and that makes the contents of the mail none of my business. I pledged $100,000 to the missionary for the work of the Lord, and asked who would join me.

After the meeting was over and the pledges were tallied, we had raised $1.8 million including my hundred grand.

Within six months the Lord brought me close to $3 million in cash, and I made my Mexico pledge good along with the others. Why had I let the $100,000 scare me while standing on that balcony in Cabo? From the time the pledge was made until the time I was able to make it good was a long six months of hard-fought battles in arguably the worst economy since the Great Depression, but that didn't stop God. He performed many miracles on my behalf and brought me through. He has never let me down. He will never let you down. Don't ever quit on Him because He will never quit on you.

These are the last days. I believe that. The signs are all around us. God needs people who are prepared to move on a task when He gives it to them. People He can trust. Those who have an internal spiritual clock know the time is short and the work has to be done now. It doesn't matter to God where you've been or who you were; the only thing that matters is who you are now. God wants you to go with Him. Follow Him and He will strengthen you. He has been planning your life since before you were born, a life of faith that brings Him honor.

4 • Self Deception

If there's nothing unresolved between you and God, you can depend on His guidance when you are following Him. Sometimes God allows a failure now to enable you to succeed later, much like any good father on the earth would do. If your child is headed for trouble by their actions or behavior, the last thing you do is to give them more money. It's like throwing gasoline on a fire. Not even a dumb dad would do that, and God is not dumb.

I've had my Heavenly Father stop my flow of income with a sledge hammer when I'm living in a way that is inconsistent with His Word. The good news is when you plant a seed, He will never give your blessing to someone else. He'll just hold it for you, put it on ice, until the blessing won't harm you or others.

The disciples all failed Jesus, and that was by design. He allowed them to fail early to enable them to succeed later. To learn from an early mistake you first have to recognize that it was a mistake. If you can't do this you won't succeed later, because the same mistake will keep taking you down.

Taking what isn't yours is wrong and a big mistake. This is a universal truth in every culture. If you build your life around the idea that stealing is okay, and never let the consequences of that idea change your mind, don't expect your later years to be successful. Stealing from God affects your destiny and future, but that truth can't help you if you don't recognize it. Any truth left unapplied has no power to guide or direct you.

Is it okay to steal from God because He is not a *real* person? What kind of person would steal from their earthly father? What's the difference? What does the way you're living say about your faith in God? These questions, if answered honestly, can remove the cloud of self-deception and put you on track to succeed later and find your destiny.

A businessman man who owned a store hired his son to work for him. The store owner was a very successful and godly man who took a portion of what he made each month to help the poor and others in need. One day the businessman realized that the store wasn't making as much profit as it had in the past, even though his sales volume had not decreased. He no longer had the funds available from his store to help the poor. The man decided that someone must be stealing from him. He installed a hidden video camera during the night when no one was around. The man waited a month before reviewing the recording in the privacy of his office. While the man watched the video his heart sank. Every Friday night at closing time, his very own son took money from the store cash box. The father's heart was broken. He loved his son very much, and had showed his son great favor in appointing him manager of his store. He'd trusted him with everything he had, and *this* was how his son chose to treat him.

It was a family tradition to meet every Sunday for lunch at the father's house, and all of his children gathered there each week. These were sad times for the father as he waited for his son to own up to what he had been doing. He didn't want to confront his son or make him look bad in front of the rest of the family. Every Sunday the father hoped that would be the day the son confessed to the thefts and said he was sorry. He wanted to forgive his son and begin the process of healing, of restoring his son to a relationship of trust. But first the son had to stop what he was doing.

Many months went by and the son continued to steal from the father. Their relationship suffered greatly. After a while the father didn't hear much of what his son had to say at the family gathering on Sundays, because the one thing he wanted to hear from his son was never mentioned. The unspoken theft lay between father and son like an invisible barrier. Eventually the father couldn't allow the son to work for him anymore, even though he loved his son with all his heart.

The most loving father in the world will not employ a son he cannot trust. You can be a near perfect child in every area of your life, but that doesn't excuse theft from your Father. Good living does not excuse bad giving. If you want to work for God to further His Kingdom and fulfill your destiny, you cannot cheat God.

> *Should people cheat God? Yet you have cheated me! But you ask, 'What do you mean? When did we ever cheat you?' You have cheated me of the tithes and offerings due to me.* (Malachi 3:8, NLT)

Some have deceived themselves into thinking that taking from God what is His (ten percent) is not theft. That thinking seems crazy to me, but with wrong perceptions we can justify crazier things than that. If we can't confront ourselves with the facts and reality of the situation then no one else can either. You can't change what you are unwilling to confront. The worst place a person can be is the place of self-deception. There is no coming back from that state unless God pulls the blinders off through circumstances that force you to face the real truth—the truth that is separate from the one you have manufactured in your mind. We fall prey to many self-deceptions and they all have a common theme: there is an element of self at the center of them and not God. The self-deceived believe that following their own guidelines contrary to the Word of God will result in greater prosperity and happiness. Like any good self-deception, obtaining the end result always appears to be much easier and faster by doing it your way instead of God's way. It's an old deception that started in the Garden of Eden, and it is designed for one thing: to erase you from God's plan and destroy your destiny. Your enemy wants you living outside of God's protection where he can raise his hand against you. He wants to minimize your life so you can't minimize his.

The thief's purpose is to steal and kill and destroy. My

purpose is to give them a rich and satisfying life. (John 10:10, NLT)

The truth left unapplied can't help or save you. Jesus Christ is the way, the truth and life. If a person doesn't apply that truth to their life then it can't save them. This is true of everything in God's Word.

In many instances people know the truth but then stop following it, so the truth we *know* becomes the truth we *knew* and it can no longer guide us. This is latent self-deception, and those who are arrogant and wealthy are most susceptible to it. These are people who know and understand the truth of God's Word but for one reason or the other start thinking it doesn't apply to them.

It's like a guy who runs along the ocean for five miles every day. Each day he runs past a sign posted on the fence that reads, "Danger! Severe Undertow! Do Not Swim!" He knows the sign is true and he believes it every morning when he runs by it, and he never considers climbing over the fence to go down for a swim.

Then one day the guy takes up swimming because all that running is really hurting his back. He heads down to the local YMCA and starts swimming every morning instead of running. At first he can't swim very far or for very long, but after a while he is swimming five miles a day. After a few years of swimming every morning he decides he'd like to get back to the outdoors and start running again. Back to the beach he goes.

The man starts running again on his old trail. One nice, sunny morning he decides to mix in some swimming with his running. He stops next to the fence with the "Danger! Severe Undertow! Do Not Swim!" sign. It's a good place to access the water. He isn't worried about the sign's warning like he used to be. After all, he has two years of training and experience now.

The day he decides to cross the fence and go past that sign is the day he dies, because the truth of the sign lost its power to save him. The ocean never stopped being dangerous at this beach; the guy just stopped believing it was dangerous. In his mind it was dangerous for others, but not for him.

I have deceived myself many times. It's an easy thing to do. The more you want something, the easier it is to slip on a pair of rose colored glasses. If you can't find a way to confront yourself and stop, you've had it. You can't change what you won't confront. Faith and obedience to God brings victory, and disobedience brings tragedy. It is so difficult to see clearly when you are caught up in a deception of your own making. Over time, walls of protection are built around those deceptions so that no one can reach in and tear them down except God. God knows every hair on your head and He knows just the right combination of circumstances to bring about for you to have a new revelation of truth. Those circumstances are almost always painful. They can be sidestepped if you stop and line up what you're doing with the Word of God.

Who in their right mind would do anything to hurt their own kids? Yet there are thousands of people who are playing around with someone they're not married to. They are self-deceived into thinking it won't hurt their children. The point is they aren't in their right mind. They are in their self-deceived mind, and they are getting help from hell below to think it. The devil wants to hurt you so you can't hurt him.

I remember driving home on a windy winter night from a girlfriend's house on the other side of the bay from Sonoma. It was about two in the morning and I wasn't thinking about too much except getting home. I had rededicated my life to God and was working my way through shedding things I had allowed into my life that I knew were not pleasing to Him. I was at peace for the first time in a long time.

I had a new gold Porsche and with no other cars or cops in sight I gave into the siren's song of letting the Porsche get up and breathe a little. Before me lay a ten-mile stretch of straight road, so I nudged the throttle and gave her a nod. We quickly became man and machine, perfectly matched in horsepower and harmony. The sounds of the whining engine tore through the night air and echoed across the choppy waters of the San Pablo Bay.

It had rained hard the previous few days and both sides of the highway were flooded with tidal pools about twenty feet deep. The flooded waters were actually wetlands attached to the San Francisco Bay on both sides of the road. When a big winter storm rolled through the area and it rained a lot, the water on the south side of the road became part of San Pablo Bay. The wind blew so hard that night I saw whitecaps foaming on top of the water in the dim light that shone from the sides of the headlights. The Porsche didn't mind the wind. It blew straight down the road at us and the faster we went the lower she crouched, like a cat clawing its paws into a Persian rug

As I passed a buck thirty, I noticed some gravel on the road. Strange that it hadn't been kicked off the road by traffic. Normally Highway 37 is a busy road. What had happened to put the gravel on the road? I started to rein the Porsche in when I caught a glimpse out of my driver's side window. A dim red light glowed at the surface of the water. It seemed kind of spooky, and I wondered what it was for a second. Then I realized it must be a car that went off the road and into the bay. That would also explain the gravel.

I backed completely out of the throttle and started shifting gears downward and braking until I was slow enough to make a U-turn. I had probably covered a quarter mile by the time I got stopped and turned around. Once I got her pointed downwind I gave the Porsche everything she had to get back there as quickly as I could.

I pulled up and stopped next to some skid marks that I hadn't noticed on my first pass and looked down at the eerie glow on the water. I couldn't make out what kind of car it was but I thought someone might still be in there, fighting for their life. I knew that time was a factor and even though I didn't know anything about emergency procedures or reviving a dead body, I did know if someone wanted to live they were going to need to breathe some air.

I strained my eyes against the wind and darkness in both directions hoping someone was on that highway and for a second I remembered how happy I was a few moments earlier when there were no cops in sight. I wished there was a cop there now. The road was empty and looked like a black asphalt parking lot with only the howl of the wind and the deafening silence of the guy inside me that should have already been in the water to help the people down there. I felt the weight of my hypocrisy that dwelt deep within me while I stood there on dry ground and stared into the dark waters while somebody was dying below me.

I thought I was the guy who would burst into a burning building to save someone. My perception of myself was the guy who would jump into a raging river to rescue a drowning kid. There was no doubt in my mind that I'd take a bullet for a buddy. I didn't think I needed courage; I thought that courage was my middle name. Turns out at this moment in time, when I was called to the line, I wasn't any of those guys. I was a scared man who didn't want to die and I just never knew it.

If anyone had told me I didn't have courage, I wouldn't have listened. What anyone had to say on the subject of courage would not have applied to me, because I thought I was the guy with courage. If I'd been asked about my courage my answers would have been wrong. That's what happens when you're self-deceived, you answer honest questions wrong.

When you're confronted with who you really are, you have a choice. You can dig in and resist the truth, trying to maintain your façade, or you can do something about it. I had to admit on this windy dark night while standing on the edge of the bay, I was scared and lacked the courage to do anything about it. I didn't like how it made me feel, and I didn't like who it made me out to be, and I wished I was anywhere but on this stretch of Highway 37 that had turned into a nightmare.

I don't know how long I stood there alone, braced against the wind and staring at this watery gravesite. It felt like a lifetime but it was probably less than a minute. It seemed as though I was in a mental freeze or something, with a million thoughts racing through my mind at the same time. It's probably the same feeling someone gets when they're told that they're adopted. They don't feel less loved by the parents who raised and cared for them but, suddenly everything they thought about who they are changes in a moment.

Once the facts settled in my mind, I knew the truth. I was a man with no courage. And I was ready to do something about it. I was ready to confront the fear that was making me who I was.

I pulled my coat off and kicked my shoes into the dirt and, forgetting to take my wallet out of my pants, jumped. When I hit the water it was so cold it felt like my heart stopped and I could barely breathe. I was so caught up in the thought of getting into the water that I didn't think about how cold the bay water was going to be. I floated there a moment, treading water and trying to steady my breathing while I got myself focused on the job at hand. Once I got adjusted to the cold so I could breathe, I started the business of trying to hold my breath so I could dive down to the submerged vehicle.

I tried two or three times to hold my breath and swim down but I didn't get more than three of four feet before I was out of breath. My heart was beating like a hummingbird's. I tried two or three times more but it soon became evident that my mind was writing checks my body just couldn't cash.

I looked up at the overcast sky with the wind slapping waves into my face and got a glimpse of a full moon between multiple layers of dark clouds. Holding my head back above the chop of the waves, my vision blurred with tears and my desperation to help turned into a resignation of failure. My heart was breaking with the knowledge that I had failed the people twenty feet below me and what that said about who I really was. I was a guy who could not be counted on in a time of need.

It seemed all that was left to do was to swim back to the road in defeat before I lost my strength and ended up dying there too. I took two strokes towards the bank and stopped. What if I made the bank and saved myself? Could I live with the knowledge that I'd saved myself and left the others below? I would never be the same again. I treaded water for a few more seconds and then came to a conclusion: I'd rather be a dead man than a live coward. The option of leaving the bay that night without diving down into that vehicle was taken off the table.

I looked back towards the full moon that was about to disappear behind the cloud cover again and cried out to the Living God. "Please help me, God! Please help me, Jesus, to be the man I want to be and not the man I am."

Suddenly the wind that had blown without ceasing completely stopped. The night grew very quiet and dead calm. I'm not sure if it was God who stopped the wind just for me or if it was just finished blowing for the night, but I'm very sure that the next thing that happened to me was all Him. As I hung there suspended in this murky sea water I felt a surge of power pierce through my whole body. Without thinking I took one big breath and dove down like an otter, descending to the bottom near the driver's door of the vehicle. It turned out to be a pick-up truck and I could feel through the dark sea water that the window was open. I pulled myself into the cab, feeling along the dash and seats looking for a body. I wasn't out of breath and I wasn't scared. I felt like I could have stayed down there for twenty minutes.

By this time I knew anyone who was in the truck would be dead. There was no air in there to breathe and it had been a good ten minutes since I first got out of my car back up on the road. I thought maybe whoever I found down there could be revived by somebody who knew what they were doing because the water was so cold, so I kept looking. When I reached the far side of the truck I hit against what felt like a body crumpled under the passenger side dash on the floor board. I grabbed hold and pulled them through the cab back to the driver's side window and started my assent to the surface.

The body was very heavy and pulling it took all I had, but it didn't matter. I was committed and I wasn't looking for a way out. The harder it got the harder I gripped and pulled my way up. I had been underwater for at least a minute when my mouth pierced through the surface and I took a half a breath of air along with a gulp of salt water. While I was struggling to keep myself afloat and dragging the body towards the shore, I heard someone shout to me from up on the road, "Are you okay!? How many of you are down there!? Hang on I'll throw you a rope!"

A man in a truck had seen my car and the skid marks and stopped while I was underwater. I wasn't going to wait for him or his rope and I wasn't in a place to have a conversation so I continued trying to make the bank, dragging the body through the water behind me. As I got closer to the shore the body began to breach the surface of the water in the darkness. I wasn't looking forward to seeing what kind of condition it would be in. I began to feel the edges of the muddy bottom skip across my toes and knew I was almost home. The man in the truck suddenly reappeared, threw a rope from above, and shouted for me to grab on. I did, and pulled myself to the bank with one hand while still clinging to the body with my other. When I finally got close enough for a firm footing in the bay mud I let go of the rope and pulled the body with all my might. I threw it onto the bank above me and then fell down to my hands and knees.

The man came down the bank with a flashlight to help and when he got there I could see that the body in front of me wasn't actually a body at all. It was a large military duffle bag full of wet clothes.

I was so exhausted that I forgot about being cold and I figured I may as well drag the bag up to the road. I got the wet duffle bag up to the highway, put it next to the Porsche that was still idling, and sat on it. The guy in the truck thought I was in the wreck and wanted to know where the Porsche driver was. I told him that I was the Porsche driver who went in after the people in the water, but there wasn't anybody down there.

The California Highway Patrol showed up a few moments later and I was still sitting on the bag. He asked me if I had been drinking and I said no and explained to him what had just gone down. The cop went to his trunk and gave me a blanket, and then invited me into his cruiser for a hot cup of coffee where he got more details of my story. Once he began to realize that my story was true he thanked me for my caring and courage. Little did the cop know what a coward I was a half hour before. Little did I know either. I left the officer with the duffle bag I saved and the mystery of where the driver was, and headed home.

My buddies that know the story still give me a bad time and kid me about saving duffle bags. I guess I've got that coming. The significance of what God did for me that night has never been lost in my mind or in my spirit. If you don't know you have a flaw in your belief of who you think you are, it can't be addressed. If it can't be addressed it can't be changed. I learned that night if I faced who I really was and didn't like what I saw God would help me change it. All I had to do was ask Him.

I was tired but full of joy that night when I drove home in my wet boxers, bare feet and green Highway Patrol blanket over my shoulders. The heater was turned all the way up to thaw my frozen body, but my soul was wrapped and warm, completely satisfied with His presence, His peace and His love. God heard my cry that night and answered my prayer. He didn't leave me as I was. He didn't leave me to live the rest of my life like that. He didn't leave me as the man I didn't want to be. He saved me that night because He loves me. He has saved me every time I have ever asked Him to, and He watches over me and protects me from my enemies.

Then call on me when you are in trouble, and I will rescue you, and you will give me glory. (Psalm 50:15, NLT)

You may not have to face an ocean free-dive in the middle of the night to find your self-deceptions, but when you are confronted with the truth that they exist in your life it will take courage to change them.

God is waiting to help you. He has a plan that is custom made just for you to insure your success. But you'll never see His plan until you're willing to confront the deception that is making you who you don't want to be.

5 • Time in Prison

Whenever someone mentioned prison ministry in my church my wallet was always open. Men would ask for my help in ministering to inmates, but there was no way I ever wanted to go anywhere near a prison. As long as I helped financially I hoped I wouldn't ever have to go in there myself. I was involved in ministries to businessmen, and prison was definitely not something I felt led to do. Nobody but God should tell you what you're called to do and if you feel led by the Holy Spirit in one direction or the other, that's what you should do. I didn't know anybody or feel led to find anybody who was in prison, or in prison ministry. It simply was not on my radar.

I was in my twenties living alone in a small cabin in Schellville. I was sitting next to the fire late one night, going over and over a story in the New Testament that bothered me. I had the feeling I was missing something. I found out early on in serving God that He usually speaks to me with questions, and He usually does it through small things. I've learned to pay attention to His Word in the little things and

and my time reading short sections of the Bible rather than trying to cover entire chapters and books. In the Bible Jesus was always asking people questions to get them to consider what they were thinking and what they were doing, and He still does that today.

The section that troubled me was Luke 10:30-37, the story of the Good Samaritan. The message seemed clear, but there was something else there I wasn't seeing. I read it slowly many times over and waited for the Lord to speak to me. After a few hours and several more logs on the fire the question came to me: "Who was the man left in the ditch for dead?"

I said, "Lord the story doesn't say. It just says some guy and it doesn't say who he was or what he was doing there on that road." I sat there waiting to hear what God would say next, and He asked the same question again. "Who was the man left in the ditch for dead?"

I stood up and walked around the one-room cabin with a dumb look on my face for a while, and then I went and stared in the refrigerator, but there was no answer to be found there. I returned to my chair, still puzzling. What was that guy doing there on the road? Where was he going when he got jumped? Was he in a bad part of town? Was he looking for hookers? Was he lost or drunk? Was he a good guy or a bad guy? The more I read the story the more evident it became that it didn't matter what he was doing there on the side of that road. What mattered was that he needed help and that's why the story didn't say. But that still didn't answer the question of who the man was, or who God wanted him to be to me.

I stared up at the beams and rafters and the only

sound in the cabin was the snap and pop of the burning logs in the fireplace. Then the Lord dropped the words into my mind and spirit: "He is like a prisoner." I leaned over and adjusted the lamp next to my chair so I could read the story again. "Why is he like a prisoner, Lord?" I asked. He answered, "The man's had everything taken from him and has been left for dead."

While I was considering the implications of what I had just heard, the Lord asked me another question. "Which one of the three men in the story do you want to be like?"

When I heard the question I fell to the floor and my heart began to melt inside of me. I squeezed my face into the palms of my hands trying to block a sudden and horrible truth the question had revealed to me about myself. I had been masquerading as a guy who cares …but I didn't. The truth was harsh and ugly: God had been drawing me to prison when men in that ministry had asked for help, but I was unwilling. I had deceived myself into believing that I had other things to do for God, and in that I was just like the priest who stepped around the guy and went to the other side of the road, not stopping to help the man left for dead. Jesus instantly changed my perception of me with a question and it was painful.

After a few minutes of shock and shame I pulled my hands from my face and stood up. The room was still the same, filled with rugs and chairs and a small fire, but somehow it now seemed lonelier. There was less me and who I thought I was to fill the space. I walked over to the fire and knelt before God and prayed. "I'm so sorry, Lord, that I'm not like the Samaritan. Please forgive me for crossing to the other side of the road. God, please let me be like the Samaritan."

I leaned my head against the wall next to a small window where I could hear the Schellville wind blowing in the night outside. I didn't know if God would speak to me or not. I stood there in silence for a while before the Holy Spirit said, "You will be like the Samaritan. Now sleep."

I felt like a man who had just won a marathon. I was so happy, but also so tired. What started out as wanting to read my Bible for a few hours after work had turned into an all night life changing event. The clock said it was almost three in the morning!

It seemed like I had just hit the pillow when my phone rang. It was still dark outside. I picked up the phone and the voice on the other end of the line said, "Hello, can I talk to Ben Hardister?" I said, "Yeah this is he." The man said his name was Ed and that he hoped I didn't mind him calling so early but he was told I was an early riser. Ed had no idea that I had only been asleep for three hours. I said, "No problem, Ed. What can I do for you?"

"Ben, I'm working on a program that brings volunteers into San Quentin Prison. We desperately need guys to come into the prison and minister to the inmates. I was hoping you'd be willing to meet with me and talk about becoming involved."

I jumped out of bed with the phone in my hand and said, "Yeah I'll do it. Where and when can we meet?" Ed paused for a minute, surprised at my quick response because he had grown accustomed to being put off by people. Very few people want to go into San Quentin Prison, and everybody there wants to get out. "Where and when would you like to meet?" Ed asked and then I said, "Let's meet right now." He started laughing and said it was pretty early and that he was over the hill in Fairfield. I said, "How about I meet you half way at the Village Bakery in Napa in an hour?" Ed thought that was a good idea, and we agreed to meet at eight o'clock. I'm pretty sure Ed figured I had a screw loose because I didn't ask a single question about the ministry; I just wanted to get in there. Nobody is that jacked up about going into San Quentin so he must have figured I was a little nuts.

It's amazing the feeling you get when you know you are in the center of God's will. There is nothing like it, and the fact that doubt and fear can rob you of this Holy Ghost experience is a real tragedy. Even though my encounter with Jesus was only a few hours old and Ed's call was an answer to my prayer to be like the Samaritan, I had all kinds of second thoughts on my way to the meeting. What did I know about prison ministry? How was I going to find the time? I soon realized that all my doubts were being driven by the physical man, not the spiritual man. None of this made any sense in the natural. I had to follow the supernatural if I was going to let God make me like the Samaritan. The spiritual man has to walk by faith because you can't put physical pieces into a spiritual puzzle; they don't fit. If all the pieces are already in place and the picture is done, you don't need any faith in what the picture will be, and then you don't need God either.

And it is impossible to please God without faith. Anyone who wants to come to him must believe that God exists and that he rewards those who sincerely seek him. (Hebrews 11:6, NLT)

Even though God spoke to me about the Samaritan not six hours earlier, the deceiver had already begun to work on me as I pulled into the parking lot of the bakery. It felt as though the words I spoke to God when I asked Him to make me like the Samaritan were already fading. Words of faith have no shelf life. Unless there is action to go with your words of faith, the words will die. Action is like a preservative for the words you speak. It keeps them alive.

What good is it, dear brothers and sisters, if you say you have faith but don't show it by your actions? Can that kind of faith save anyone? (James 2:14, NLT)

I met Ed sitting in the bakery and after a few minutes it was evident that he had a passion for the lost. He told me about the needs in the prison and shared his commitment to God and the inmates. Ed asked why I was so excited about prison ministry and how long I had been considering it. I told him I'd been thinking about getting involved in the prison ministry for about six or seven hours. We both started laughing. Over breakfast I told him of my encounter with Jesus the night before, and when we were finished we set a time to meet at San Quentin. Ed and I became good friends and he was a great source of inspiration to me. I ended up traveling with Ed to many prisons in other countries as well as the U.S.

If Ed had called me a day earlier I would have come up with any excuse I could think of to stay away from San Quentin, and done so with a clear conscience because I didn't think prison ministry had anything to do with me. Now I was prepared to do anything to get into San Quentin. What happened? God showed me a different perspective to change the direction of my life using His Word. Now I needed to do something about it and not just have a conversation about it. I didn't need to discuss the truths I had learned. I didn't need to go buy some books about bringing significance to life from success in business, or some other drivel read by men who do nothing. I didn't need to wait until I'd been trained or 'empowered' by attending workshops and conferences; I was already empowered by God's Word to me and the only thing I lacked was getting out and getting to it. There's nothing wrong with men supporting each other in God's work, but that's not an excuse to delay putting your faith into action. Don't ever fall for the idea that knowing about something is the same as doing something. Fluffy dogs can tell you all about how to do something but they've never done anything themselves except bark. These people sit around with itching ears and in their arrogance think they are doing God a favor because they acknowledge Him with their words while doing nothing with their hands or their checkbooks.

Ed arranged for me to go into the prison a few weeks later. The process of getting into a prison is kind of involved because of the security of keeping guys in there from getting out. San Quentin Prison was built in the 1800's and actually started as a floating prison barge anchored to Point San Quentin for prisoners during the Gold Rush days.

After spending some time in the chapel, I headed out to the tiers with two volunteers who were there that day. They were two older guys that I'm guessing were close to seventy and they spent the whole day once a week walking the tiers. They pushed a big cart that resembled what a restaurant busboy fills with dishes, only this cart was full of various types of greeting cards that the two men offered to the inmates.

The prison tiers are different levels of cages that are stacked inside a warehouse five stories high. Volunteers from the chapel would push the cart through the open yard to old buildings known as *sections*, or *blocks*. Once you arrive at a cell block there is an identification process that takes place, moving you from one locked area to the next. Once inside the building, it is a two-man operation to lift and pull the card cart up the stairs to each level. Then it is pushed down the tier, stopping in front of each man's cell.

I followed one of the guys around and listened to his conversation with the inmates. I was trying to get a handle on what to expect. These two volunteers made their way through the cell block that day, pausing to talk with every man who wanted to talk. They asked every inmate if they wanted a greeting card and then asked if they had ever prayed the sinner's prayer. This went on all day until they finished walking the entire block, all five stories.

Dark was starting to fall as we left the cell block heading back to the chapel, and fog swirled around the old stone and steel structures. The sound of men yelling and cursing pierced the heavy night air and I wondered how these men could be reached for Christ. After spending the day in this place walking by each cell, it didn't seem like I was in the right place or with the right plan.

When we made it back to the chapel one old fella asked the other, "How many salvations did you get today?" The guy answered, "Thirteen." Then the first guy said, "Oh man that is great. You beat me again, I only prayed with eight today."

These two guys were the salt of the earth who loved Jesus and showed it in faith and action. They were walking the tiers when they could have been safe and warm at home and I admired them for that, but the way they were going about their ministry was not for me. I knew from my encounter with the Holy Spirit while reading about the Good Samaritan and the meeting with Ed that God wanted me to go to the prisoner or the man left in the ditch for dead, but I felt like this was the wrong way to go about it. I knew I was pursuing the right ministry but maybe it was the wrong place. I needed to get some further instructions.

I thanked everybody at the chapel and headed for the main security gate to exit San Quentin Prison, figuring I wouldn't be back. As I was waiting my turn to enter the security chamber to leave, a guy came through from the free side and stopped to say hello. "Where are you coming from?" he asked. I told him I was coming from the Garden Chapel and he asked if I had been there all day. I said that I was. His eyes lit up and he said, "Man that's great, it's good to see a young guy in here who wants to minister to the inmates." He introduced himself as a new chaplain at the Garden Chapel. His name was Earl.

Earl asked, "So are you going to be coming in on a weekly basis? Will I see you next week? What's your name, man?" He had a big smile on his face and his excitement about his new job was obvious. I didn't want to lie to the guy so I said, "My name is Ben, and I'm not going to lie to you, Preacher. I won't be coming back in here." The chaplain was taken back and asked me why not. I liked Earl right away. We were about the same age and in the first few seconds of sizing him up you could tell he had been around and could handle himself. Earl had come from the streets of Stockton, California, where he had to grow up fast and found plenty of trouble. He found Jesus, dedicated his life to serve Him, enrolled at Golden Gate Theology Seminary and became a chaplain.

Earl walked me over towards the chapel and asked, "Why don't you want to come back, man, did something happen?" I said, "Listen, Preacher. I'm a businessman and develop real estate. I don't know anything about prisons or prison ministry and I'm not going to tell you how to do things. I'm just not interested in doing things the way they're being done here." He gave me a serious look. "I'd like to hear what you have to say. What would you do different?"

I looked at this guy and could tell he was sincere and wasn't just asking me for my opinion so he could hammer me about how wrong I was. I said, "Well, I can't reach four hundred individual men for Christ in an eight hour day, and I sure as heck don't think I have the right to ask some guy if he's prayed the sinners prayer after knowing him for thirty seconds. Pushing around a cart with cards and asking everyone to pray the sinner's prayer is not something I can abide with." Earl stared at me for a moment and then pointed at me. "How would you do it?" I said, "Come on man, I'm not going to get into that." But he wouldn't let me off the hook. He pointed at me again and said, "I want to know, how would you do it?" So I said, "I can't help four hundred guys, but I could help twenty. If I had twenty guys that I could get to know and earn the right to their trust and respect, I could reach them for Christ."

Earl paused for a time then stepped closer to me. "Okay, I hear you, but let's just say you only talk to these twenty guys and you do reach them for Christ. What about the other 5,980 men?" Without thinking about what I was saying I answered him. "Preacher, if the Holy Ghost is behind what I'm saying, I'll get 300 guys into this prison we'll and rock this place for Jesus!" Earl slapped my arm and started laughing. "You might be right, Ben, but it would have to be a miracle of God to get twenty volunteers to come in here every week, let alone three hundred." I just smiled. "I am right, Preacher, and it's got nothing to do with me."

We both started laughing and Earl said, "Alright, Brother, you come back next week and I'll give you twenty guys to talk to that aren't going anywhere."

The following week on Wednesday I left at seven o'clock in the morning for San Quentin. Earl met me at the front gate and took me into the chapel. After an hour or so of getting to know one another, Earl said, "You ready to go, Brother?" I said, "Yep," and away we went. Ten minutes later we were at cell block "C" or "Carson Section." C Block was on the southern end of the prison property. This place seemed real different than the prison section I was at the week before, and there were two locked areas to pass through instead of one. The building stood on the very edge of the San Francisco Bay with the sea water lapping just below the outside wall. You could tell by the twenty coats of paint that the building had been there for a long time.

When we entered the main line of the cell block

there were no inmates standing around outside their cells like there had been at the other cell block. All of the men were locked down in their cells, and there seemed to be more officers in this place. High above our heads suspended in the air was a catwalk with an officer holding a rifle in his hands, looking down at us.

Earl walked me up the metal stairs five stories high to a locked gate in the center of the tier. We stood there, staring through the bars at the prisoners in their dark cells. While we waited for the tier officer to come and unlock the gate I was trying to process everything I was seeing. What in the world had the Lord put me in the middle of?

While standing there five stories in the air on the open stairway, I caught a glimpse of a ferry boat making its way across the bay to San Francisco through a small window on the outside wall. The outside world looked dim and far away through air thick with smoke from hundreds of cigarettes and burning toilet paper.

Many of the inmates had tightly rolled toilet paper the size of thick dental floss coiled and stacked at the bottom of their cell doors with the upper end lit and hanging over the cell's cross bar. As the toilet paper would smolder and burn into ash the inmate would pull down additional lengths allowing it to burn back up to the cross bar. These tightly rolled coils of burning toilet paper smoldered for hours a day and the convicts used the burning ends to light their homemade cigarettes.

I'd driven to the prison in bright sunshine, but the inside of this dungeon was dark and gloomy while we stood there and waited for an officer to open the gate.

Suddenly there was a shout behind us that startled me. It came from the guy with the rifle on the catwalk who was at the same level as we were five stories in the air. "Man at the gate!" he yelled to the officer at the end of the tier. A minute later the guard showed up and opened the gate. Earl stayed on the outside of the gate as I walked in, and he closed the gate behind me. I looked at him like a kid who just got left in a dark parking lot, watching his dad drive away. "What are you doing man?" I asked. "I'll be back to get you for lunch around noon," he said, and down the stairs he went, leaving me standing on the west side of the tier in front of twenty locked cells.

I didn't know it then, but Earl had left me with twenty men who had been condemned to die in the gas chamber. I was on Death Row at San Quentin.

When the Holy Spirit spoke to me a month earlier in my cabin and told me that the man left in the ditch for dead in the story of the Good Samaritan was like a prisoner left for dead, He meant it literally. I had thought that any man in prison was left for dead, and in many cases that's true. But these men had been *sentenced* and left for dead.

Earl and I became best friends and still are today. He married me and my wife, and he has always been there when I needed him. It took us only a few months to recruit twenty guys (mostly buddies of mine) and within a year we had fifty. Then several hundred. Within a few years we reached the point that every twenty inmates had someone ministering to them personally, and Jesus did rock that prison just like He said He would. Our program became one of the largest prison ministries of its kind in the United States. Earl ran the spiritual stuff with training the volunteers and dealing with the State of California, and eventually the Lord put me in the role of making money to pay the bills. We had a weekly TV show inside the prison on closed cable and I hired a full time administrator to correct Bible studies and track volunteers and inmates. We bought every prisoner in the house who did our studies a leather study Bible, and gave them T-Shirts as well. We bought TV's for guys who didn't have one and helped to bring family members in when an inmate was executed. We saw dozens of men accept Christ as their Savior on death row and thousands of men gave their hearts to Christ in the rest of the prison.

I was making good enough money in my real estate development business to pay for everything and God was blessing everything I did. I wasn't spending a tithe of my income because ten percent would not have been nearly enough to pay for everything. I was spending what was needed to float the program, and the Lord blessed me over and above that to take care of my own bills including building a new house in the hills above Sonoma. My faith was in God and God was being honored by the things we were doing. We were dogs that could hunt when the Lord sent us out, and we found the men hidden in the brush and brought them back to the Master.

Earl and I had worked together for almost ten years and during that period I somehow got the idea that God needed me to fund His ministry, therefore He had to keep blessing me regardless of how I lived my life. I was about to learn one of the most important lessons of my life. I was already convinced and understood that "Good living does not excuse bad giving," but I was about to be educated on the flip side of that truth in a very painful way. I think it's more difficult to understand the truth that, "Good giving does not excuse bad living." It has to be harder because I've had to learn it more than once, and I don't want to believe that I am that stupid.

I could say it was the heartbreak of being around for the executions at San Quentin when they started up again with Robert Harris. I had seen Robert every week for almost ten years and had led him to the Lord. Earl and I had started a Bible Study in the visitor's room for condemned inmates each week on Wednesday. What a sight it was! Twenty condemned men chained to each other around a table reading scriptures about Jesus and His love for them while twenty officers stood by as guards in case they tried to escape. Robert was one of the men at that table and when it came time for him to go suck the fumes from that box, he appointed me as his religious advisor. I guess I wasn't ready for the heat that followed. These men had all smoked the pipe of murder and they all had what was coming to them one way or the other. They were condemned to die in the Gas Chamber, but they hadn't been condemned to die in hell yet as long as they were still breathing. They were no different than the men you see on the street. We all have it coming for the things we've done, but while we're still breathing we can be born again (born a second time) and pardoned from a permanent death in hell if we only ask to be forgiven and repent. If you're only born once you die twice, but if you're borne twice you only die once. We had to get to know these men to share Jesus with them. It's hard to know a man for years and then one day shake his hand and watch him walk away to the Gas Chamber.

Or maybe it was the pressure of business and funding all the financial needs that caused me to stray from a straight path. I could say it was the constant problems from other Christians who were always trying to tear the ministry down. I wanted to be free from the heartache and responsibility for other people's lives and eternity. I didn't want to be a hunting dog anymore. Along the line somewhere I had taken what belonged to God and put it on my own door step where it didn't belong, and it tore my heart up. I knew that Jesus could take it from me but I thought I could handle it if I just had a break. The truth is I thought I deserved a break. I wanted to mess around and have some fun and some beer and I figured God would look the other way because He needed me. My thinking was twisted up and I had sold myself on the idea that what I was doing didn't matter because I was a special case because I had been through so much, I was above the law. I had become self-deceived, and with my perspective and attitude I wasn't going to make it unless God pulled some strings and saved me.

God told Joshua to mediate day and night on His Word and only then would he succeed (Joshua 1:6-9). Two things there I missed. The first is there are no breaks. You take a break and you're going down. The second is this is the *only* way to succeed. You can't come up with another way outside of His Word. It won't work.

I was no different than the guy who convinces himself that he can be blessed and accepted by God while stealing from God. When you're self-deceived and sold on false ideas, nobody can talk any sense into you. Why do you think it's called *self*-deception?

It begins with self and it's something that self wants. There can't be any self-deception if you get rid of self. Bringing honor and glory to God is a life that has no room for self.

Feeding self will tear you up. I convinced myself that having a girlfriend while I was married wasn't unlike the guys in the Old Testament. God had just made men that way, so it wasn't so bad. I figured Jesus turned water into wine and the Bible said something about giving drink to a man with a heavy heart, so boozing at the bar wasn't so bad either. I don't remember how I justified myself into punching people in the mouth at bar fights, but I had an angle on that too. Probably something from Ezekiel 25:17 and the vengeance of the Lord.

When I got far enough away from God's protection for the enemy to take me down, he struck all at once. In a short period of time he took everything I had. My wife and I divorced, and she left with my five- and six-year-old kids. I moved out of a million dollar home to live a 24-foot travel trailer with a leaky roof and sixty second showers. My new Mercedes and Jaguar were replaced by an old Audi with only one working door, and both my airplanes flew away to some other owner.

After spending years in prison trying to help others, I had taken my eyes off Jesus and serving Him to serve myself. Now I was in a prison of my own, one without bars on the windows. Samson didn't become physically blind until he became spiritually blind first, and I had fallen into the same trap. I'm not saying I was Samson, but I did the same thing.

Samson was a Nazirite and had taken a Nazirite Vow. A Nazirite Vow can be for a specific period of time or for an entire lifetime. Part of the vow is to never cut your hair, but when the vow is finished you cut your hair. When Samson allowed Delilah to cut his hair, he was saying to God, "I am finished serving you." He had become spiritually blind, and a short time later he became physically blind as a slave grinding at the wheel.

I did the same thing and didn't even know it. When I chose to serve myself instead of God I became spiritually blind, and a short time later I lost the things that were precious to me. I was forced to grind at the wheel of sin and debt, every bit as much a slave as Samson.

Through all of these events God showed me His mercy by not wiping me out when He had every reason to. God gave me good friends who never turned their back on me or treated me any differently when I was on the bottom than when I was on the top. I think God knows I wouldn't have made it without them. I was like the paralyzed guy on the mat in Capernaum who had four good buddies who took apart the roof to lower their friend down before Jesus. My friends did the same for me, except they took the roof off and lifted me up to Jesus. Anybody can beat the manure out of one dog and get him down. That's easy. It's a lot harder to beat down a whole pack of dogs, so make sure you're running with a good pack of hunting dogs. If the devil gets you down and starts to lay the boots to you and all you have around you are fluffy dogs, then you are in real trouble.

The Lord used the mistakes I made at that time to enable me to succeed at a later time. Was it His will that I did those things? I don't think so, but the Bible says He will take everything—or *all* things—and make them bend in the end to bring about something good for people who love Him and follow the plan He laid out for their life.

> *And we know that God causes everything to work together for the good of those who love God and are called according to his purpose for them.* (Romans 8:28, NLT)

Everything includes the bad things. I know lots of people who are like the Prodigal Son's older brother who don't like that very much. If you've messed up, some folks think you should stay in the onion cellar peeling potatoes and wiping tears all day. There's a time for that, but then you have to move on. It's like the guy who gets popped in the face and gets a broken nose. The guy who did the popping forgets about it without much trouble, but the guy who looks in the mirror and sees his crooked nose for the next fifty years never forgets and has a hard time forgiving. It doesn't matter if you're the popper or the poppee, there has to be a place at the table for both because God says there is. It seems to me that you get double-banged by not forgiving. You get the initial blow of being wronged, and then the second blow of living a life outside of God's blessings by choosing not to forgive.

> *Meanwhile, the older son was in the fields working. When he returned home, he heard music and dancing in the house, and he asked one of the servants what was going on. "Your brother is back," he was told, "and your father has killed the fattened calf. We are celebrating because of his safe return." The older brother was angry and wouldn't go*

in. His father came out and begged him. (Luke 15:25-28, NLT)

Many times God will allow someone to fail early so they can succeed later. We aren't privy to His plans, so if we fight against someone who has stumbled or hurt us in the past we may find ourselves fighting against God Himself. The devil can have the past; God owns the future. Whatever side of the equation you find yourself on, whether you have done the hurting or received the hurting, it doesn't matter. Everyone must step forward and move away from the past, nobody who God uses for His honor and glory can harbor hard feelings or unforgiveness towards someone who has messed up. It doesn't seem right that things are this way, but what seems right has got nothing to do with it. Does it seem right that a guy who works for an hour makes the same as a guy who works for eight hours? (Matthew 20:15) God's ways are not our ways. His ways are higher than ours, and if there is any bending of attitudes needed it will come from our side of the table, not His.

When you get your eyes on yourself, even if it's just for a night to say, "Hey I need a break," you are headed for a lesson you aren't going to like.

It took a few years for me to get up and brush my pants off, and then a few years more to climb out of the hole I dug. The lessons I've learned are constant reminders of how easy it is to get off track by selling yourself on an idea of something being okay when it's not. Don't think you're getting away with something just because everything is going well. Eventually something is going to break. God corrects those He loves and a correction is on the way to help you with any deception that may have wormed its way into your life. If things aren't going well, stop the madness, correct yourself and get back on track. The earlier you stop digging your hole, the shorter the climb will be getting out of that hole.

> *Do not be deceived, God is not mocked; for whatever a man sows, that he will also reap.* (Galatians 6:7, NKJV)

6 • The Exchange

You have to move before God can move. From Jesus all the way back to Abraham this has always been God's way, because it is the way of faith. Moving into the future, trusting in God's word is faith with honor. The honor comes from the moving; there is no honor in sitting or hiding. The words, "You move so I can move," came to me from the Lord when I was in a tight spot and I never forgot His message. The story of the exchange is proof of God's ability and desire to move on our behalf if we move first on His behalf, if we show by our actions that we believe and trust in Him.

I sold a thirty-seven acre property in Sonoma and decided to do an exchange into another income property in Modesto. I looked around for a few months and finally settled on a commercial building leased to a soup company that had moved from San Francisco to be more centrally located. The cap rate on the building was over eight percent and it was the best deal I could find at the time. The exchange called for a cash down payment of $1.1 million, and then financing for $1.6 million. The total purchase price was around $2,700,000.

I was a little concerned because the building was being used in a highly specialized industry making soup, and if the tenant or soup company went broke it might be hard to locate a new tenant. My concerns were erased when, as part of the deal, I negotiated a line of credit from the tenant guaranteeing me $400,000 if they defaulted on the lease. I figured if the company went belly up this would give me enough capital to do improvements for another tenant and make mortgage payments while the building was empty.

I went ahead and bought the building and eighteen months later the soup company went broke. I was left with an empty building, no rent, and $13,000 per month in mortgage and taxes.

I went down to the bank to collect on the $400,000 line of credit that was due to me according to our contract only to discover that the bank had already taken it. When I called the big shot at the bank they said they took the money because the property had less security for the loan now that there was no tenant. No kidding! That's why I included the $400,000 line of credit as part of the deal in the first place! It was not their money to take, it was mine, but the bank took it anyway. I had no recourse except to sue, which I did not want to do. I couldn't make the monthly mortgage payment. All I could do was try to sell the building, however long that took.

A few months later on New Year's Day, my wife Karen and I were at our family cabin in the Sierra Nevada Mountains and we were walking along the

Feather River in the snow. I asked the Lord what He wanted me to do in the coming year. The Holy Spirit had already told me that I was finished helping in Venezuela after my last trip, and we were curious and excited about what the new year had in store for us. I wasn't sure if the Lord would tell me, because He doesn't always answer when I ask Him to. God tells me that He loves me every morning if I listen for Him, but when I want specific answers the Holy Spirit usually leads me to the Bible and tells me to trust Him.

We had walked along the river for a half hour or so and turned back toward the cabin when the Holy Spirit spoke to me. When I say spoke, it is hard to explain. It's like a concept or picture as I've said in an earlier chapter, but sometimes it's words, that instantly pop into your mind and you know it's Him. I don't have a problem believing God can control my small mind when He controls a very large universe.

The Lord spoke to me and said, "I want you to go to Mexico, and I want you to take $100,000." I didn't have a hundred grand but that was not anything new. God frequently asks me for something I don't have. The $100,000 didn't concern me because I knew if He wanted me to give the money, He would supply it. But I wanted to know about Mexico. So I asked the Lord, "Where at in Mexico, and to who?" "Just across the border and I'll show you who," is all I heard.

When we got back to the cabin I told Karen what I thought the Lord had told me down on the river, and she had the same question for me that I had for the Lord. "Where in Mexico and to who?" We were in the middle of a financial situation that was getting worse with each passing day. It's a common dilemma that many people find themselves in when more money is going out than coming in. It sounds crazy to some people but when your needs are the greatest, it's the greatest time to meet the needs of others. I was excited about this new opportunity to give because I knew my provision for someone else's need would open God's hands to meet my needs as well.

For the next three or four months I asked every person I met if they knew of a ministry in Mexico that needed help. Nobody knew anybody and I didn't want to push it too hard because God said He would show me. I didn't want to find myself helping the wrong ministry because I forced something to happen.

Sometime around April I made a few bucks, but not enough to pay off the bank for the soup company building. Instead I bought a property next to the local high school for a church and youth center. The property consisted of two houses in the back and three commercial spaces in the front. One of the commercial lots in the front contained a small church of fifty that wanted to expand into the whole space. I negotiated the purchase of the entire property with two different sellers, put the money down to buy them, and closed escrow, giving the property and mortgages to the preacher.

In the meantime I had been in a standoff with the bank on the soup company property for a while. I was well into default when I got an offer from an ice cream manufacturer to buy the property for about what I paid for it. I knew if the bank got wind of the sale they would demand all the interest payments that were due and they'd never give me back the $400,000 that was mine from the guarantee.

The bank's headquarters was in Chico so I flew up there to negotiate a settlement before they knew the property had an offer on it. At the end of a very contentious day with the bank and their lawyers, I agreed to pay the mortgage off within ninety days and the bank would forgive up to $400,000 of the delinquent monthly interest payments. But I had to agree to sign off any of my foreclosure rights as part of the deal. If I didn't pay them in full in ninety days they took the building back along with my $1 million in equity. I wasn't worried about signing my rights away because the deal I had to sell the building was solid with a $100,000 non-refundable deposit, and buyers' new loan had been approved.

Almost three months later we were only a few days from closing when the realtor called. "Ben, I've got good news and bad news. Which do you want first?" I said, "Give me the bad news," and he said, "The bank has decided not to do the loan." "What?" I yelled into the phone. "What's the good news?" And he said "You get to keep the buyers' $100,000 deposit." The realtor didn't know about the deal I made with the bank to settle the dispute. There was no good news. If the bank in Chico wasn't paid in a week I lost $1 million, so getting $100,000 back was not good news. I didn't have time to resell the property to someone else and even if I did, it was impossible to get a new commercial appraisal and loan in seven days.

It was a Friday and everything I could see with my eyes and hear with my ears told me we had just lost a million bucks. I went home, picked up my wife and took her to dinner at our favorite restaurant in Modesto. On the way I explained what had happened.

She smiled a small smile and then asked me what any sane person would ask, "What are we going to do now?" And I said, "Honey, when I was a boy my grandpa always used to tell me, 'they can take your house and car, your hunting rifle and the clothes off your back, but they can't eat you because that's illegal.'" I started laughing but she didn't think it was funny.

While at dinner we encouraged each other and talked about God's goodness and how He had always came through before. We were in the middle of dinner and Karen was talking about something unrelated to the day's train wreck when the Holy Spirit showed up and asked me, "What about Mexico?" I was stunned and dumbfounded. I couldn't believe God was bringing up Mexico at a time like this. We were in big trouble. I was expecting to hear a Word about victory over my enemies and prosperous crops or something, and He asks me about Mexico?

I had already forgotten and discarded the Word about Mexico. In my mind and spirit I thought I heard God speak to me on New Year's Day on the Feather River, but all of my efforts to find a person or ministry that needed help in Mexico had come to nothing. I assumed the Word was for a later time and had put it on the back burner knowing there was six months left in the year. I sat at this small restaurant and listened for His voice again until I heard Him say the same thing again, "What about Mexico?" I said, "God, please. Mexico? I've tried all year to find somebody in Mexico who was just across the border and there was no one and besides that, I spent all of our money buying that commercial corner for the church and youth center."

While I was having this conversation with God, Karen was talking to me about something and I didn't hear a word she was saying. It was like I was in a different dimension and she could have been talking about flying monkeys for all I knew. Then the Holy Spirit spoke to me again and said, "Don't worry about the preacher's house and church you bought, you can do more than one thing at a time. I'm training you. Now listen very carefully. You need to move so that I can move. There isn't much time and you need to move quickly so that I can move."

My head swam with His Words and I was trying to figure out what the Holy Spirit was saying to me. How could I move with no direction? I waited for a further revelation or a Word or something, and there was nothing. My eyes were fixed on a half-eaten bowl of jambalaya sitting in front of me. I glanced around the restaurant for somebody to bring me an envelope with a message, or maybe a prophet to approach and proclaim, "Thus says the Lord." Nothing. A few minutes passed while I prayed in the spirit without speaking, and then I asked God, "What do you mean Lord? How can I move? I don't have any direction to move in. Should I just leave for the border? How will I know where to go, because it's a long border? Please help me, Jesus, and give me some direction."

A moment later I thought of my daughter Natalie who had gone to an orphanage in Mexico a few years earlier with her youth group. In the same thought, my friend Jonathon who is an Assembly of God preacher came to mind. The two thoughts didn't seem to fit together, but it was at least something to go on. I jumped up from the table, grabbed my cell phone and told my wife I'd be right back.

I stepped outside the restaurant by the street so I wouldn't disturb anyone and called Jonathon. His church was up in Middletown. When he answered I asked him if he knew anybody who was working for Jesus close to the border in Mexico, maybe someone with an orphanage or something. Jonathon said, "Oh that would be Steve Horner." I asked him why he spit his name out so quickly and he said Horner was the only guy he knew in Mexico close to the border. Then I asked if he could find this Horner guy's phone number. Of course Jonathon wanted to know what this was all about. I told him I'd tell him later but that I really needed for him to see if he could find Horner's phone number.

He came back to the phone a few minutes later. He'd found the number in his denomination's directory. I wrote it down and then punched it in my cell phone right there on the street. A guy answered and I asked, "Are you Steve Horner?" It was, and we talked for about a minute while I tried to establish a connection or rapport with him, trying to figure out who he was, what he was doing, and why God was sending me to him. Steve didn't know anybody that I knew and I didn't know anybody that he knew so it was a short preliminary to the questions I really needed to ask.

After we talked for a minute Steve asked, "What's this call all about?" I said, "Steve, I have two questions for you. The first one is this: where are you located?" He said "We are just across the border in Mexico." When he said that I let out a huge sigh of relief, because that is exactly what God had told me on the Feather River. I started to feel the presence of the Holy Ghost, and said, "Second question. Can you tell me what you have need of right now?" Steve said, "Well, my son and I had a vision to build a Bible College here in Mexico next to our orphanage. We've poured a 20,000 square foot slab and framed the building, but we ran out of money a year ago. The building has been sitting as a home for the birds. If I had $100,000 I could finish the Bible College building and start educating pastors next year."

I had found the guy! What the Lord was sending me there for had nothing to do with the orphanage. It was for a Bible College. I tried to throttle back my enthusiasm before speaking because I didn't want to sound like a dork. "Okay Steve, do you know where Brown Airfield is in San Diego?" He laughed. "I hope I know where Brown Field is in San Diego. I'm looking at Brown Field out my window right now as I'm driving by it on my way back to the orphanage." Turns out he was on his way back from the airport in an old school bus after delivering a group of youth volunteers who'd spent a week helping out at the orphanage.

I told Steve that I'd be at Brown Field at noon next Friday with a cashier's check for $100,000 and asked him who I should make it payable to. The phone was silent for a moment and then Steve said, "Mister you better not be yanking my chain." I told him I wasn't, and that the money didn't have anything to do with me. I was on a mission from God and that I would have God's money there by noon next Friday. He said to make the check payable to: *Rancho De Sus Niños.*

The time from when I left the table in our favorite restaurant until the time I came back to join my wife took maybe five minutes. I sat down at the table and Karen asked me what that was all about. It took me a while to explain to her what was going on.

I explained to her that we have to move to allow God to move, and we talked about all of God's servants in the Bible that did the same thing. We are God's servants so we shouldn't expect anything different today than what he did back then during the Bible days. God is an unchanging God. It took me twenty minutes to explain to her what the Holy Spirit impressed upon me in a few moments, and then about the conversations that had just taken place outside.

When I was finished, she said, "We just lost $1 million, and now we are giving away $100,000?" I said, "Yep." My wife sat there for a few moments playing with her coffee cup, and then she looked up. "Okay, I'm with you but where are we going to get that much money?" I grinned at her. "We'll work on that next week." Then we both shared a good laugh. We were well past any financial safety net and completely in the hands of God, and that's right where He wanted us.

On Monday morning three days later I made a call to a banker friend in Sonoma and arranged a loan against some property we owned there. I'd found my hundred grand to cover the cashier's check I was taking down to Steve Horner on Friday. The same morning the realtor from Modesto called and said he had another bank who was interested in giving the buyer a loan on the soup property. I commented to him that a commercial appraiser had taken sixty days to appraise the property for the first bank, and even if this bank's appraiser could do it in half that time we still only had a week before I lost the building. The realtor said, "Yeah you're right. It would take a miracle." When he said that I suddenly realized something. It was a miracle we were looking for, *not* a natural way out. I told him to proceed with the new bank.

The next day the realtor called and said the appraiser was at the property. On Wednesday he called and said the building had appraised. On Thursday he called and said the loan was approved and going to committee. On Friday he called and said the loan was ready to fund!

If you don't know anything about commercial real estate this story probably doesn't mean much. But if you do, you know this can't happen in a normal world. It doesn't matter what business you are in or where you work, there are miracles waiting for you when you decide to trust and honor God with your actions. Words won't do it. You can sit at the table with all the words you want, but until you slap some leather on the horse and start moving nothing is going to change.

On Friday my wife and I loaded our plane with fuel and we were wheels up at 9:00 am for the two-and-a-half hour flight to Brown Field with a hundred grand for a Bible school. We met Steve at noon and gave him the check. He just sat there laughing and said, "I really thought you were a flake. But something in me hoped that you weren't, so I came down here just to see if you'd show up." He stared at that check, shaking his head. "Nobody has ever given us this much money." I told Steve the money belonged to God; we were only delivering the package. Then I said, "Horner I apologize for keeping you hanging and being late. The Lord told me about your need on New Year's day and it took me six months to find you." He replied, "I'm glad you did," and we all had a good laugh.

Steve took us into Mexico and we spent the night getting to know him and his wife Cathy over dinner at their house next to the orphanage and a half-built Bible College in the Mexican desert.

I left early the next day to have coffee with Steve and hear more about what he was doing in Mexico for the Lord. When I headed back to the small trailer where we had stayed the night before, I saw my wife Karen in the distance through the dusty grounds of the orphanage. She stood in the morning light, looking at the future Bible College. I walked down and joined her and she leaned against my shoulder and began to cry. I asked her what was wrong and she said she was moved by the work that God was doing there. She wondered where these people would be if we had not listened to God. She was beginning to understand what most people never do. She was learning a lesson from the Holy Spirit on this trip. "If God's servants don't move in faith when He speaks to them, people will always suffer."

We made friends and were able to touch many live for Jesus in Mexico. In addition to finishing the Bible College, we ended up helping them build a Hospice home and eight churches with the help of many other businessmen and friends. It would take another book just to describe half of what we saw God do in Mexico during those few short years, and what He is still doing there today.

The biggest blessing of all was learning a truth that could be applied and used and reused to keep God's abundance flowing in our lives to benefit others – you have to move before God can move. From the story of Abraham and all the way through the Bible, people had to move in faith first and then God moved. Even God's own Son Jesus had to move first before God could move.

If you consider that Jesus is part of the Trinity, you have to figure that God knows Him real well.

> *"My Father has entrusted everything to me. No one truly knows the Son except the Father, and no one truly knows the Father except the Son and those to whom the Son chooses to reveal him."* (Matthew 11:27, NLT)

God the Father knew Jesus the Son was willing to come to the earth to save mankind. God the Father knew Jesus would be successful in defeating Satan and sin by coming back from the grave, because God knows everything. So if God knew Jesus was willing to come to the earth and that Jesus would be successful when He came, why send Him down here in the first place? Why couldn't Jesus just stay there with God in Heaven and let mankind be saved based on Jesus' intentions and God's knowledge that Jesus would be successful? Jesus had to move before God could move, and anyone who thinks God is going to do for them what He would not do for His Son or the prophets is not thinking straight.

The intent of your heart without any action doesn't count for much when it comes to serving the Lord and fulfilling your destiny. It's what you do when you move forward with what is in your heart that matters

.

Photographs

Ben is the chaplain of the Soldiers of the Cross motorcycle club.

Ben and his team stopping in at Mother Teresa's to help out
while building a nursing school in Kolkata

Praying with students at a school for the blind in Kolkata

Walking the grounds of the small farm used to feed the
children at the blind school in Kolkata.

The team Ben took to Cambodia to buy land for a girls' home in
Phnom Penh (From left: David Wagner, missionary; Ben;
Nelson Cooney; Larry Hunter; Scott Monticelli; Ken Huff,
driver and missionary; Dennis Allison; Dan Fowler)

Ben with his friend, author and founder of the San Francisco
City Impact ministry Roger Huang

Speaking to students in Uganda

With a local boy while buying land for a farm in Uganda.

School and orphanage in Uganda

The Bible College in Mexico Ben financed for Steve
Horner's *Rancho de Sus Niños* ministry.

Building the road for *Rancho de Sus Niños* Bible College and Orphanage.

Ben and Steve Horner, the founder of the *Rancho de Sus Niños*. Ben spent the day operating a Cat tractor building the roads for the *Rancho* project.

The Bible College in Mexico.

Ben at the border of Uganda.

The building purchased to build the nursing school in Kolkata.

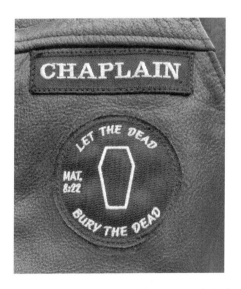

One of the patches Ben wears on his motorcycle jacket.

Photo taken at an outreach for the homeless in the Tenderloin of San Francisco. From left: Michael McDonald, UFC Mixed Martial Arts fighter; Ben; Dan Freeman, founder of Fight Labs; Ryon Tobar, California Mixed Martial Arts title holder; Christian Huang, director of the SF City Impact.

Ben and his chopper.

7 • Trusting God to save a Rescue Mission

M ost of the people who are called, or invited to the King's party, choose not to come. They don't think the King cares what they do, or what they wear, and they don't listen when the King speaks.

> *"For many are called, but few are chosen."* (Matthew 22:14, NLT)

The chosen are selected from the called. There comes a time when you have to decide to abandon human wisdom and accept spiritual wisdom or you can't go any farther down the road with God. You can accept what you can't see as fact, yield to the world of the Spirit, and travel an endless highway of excitement in the supernatural, or you can accept what you can see in the physical world and stay right where you are—on a dead end street.

If you're smart by the world's standards, it is not easy following God. Most people who are worldly smart have spent years studying what makes what work. Theirs is a world of numbers and equations, and they trust in what the equations say over what the Spirit says. I say *most* smart people, not all. It's not a very big secret that lots of kids go into college believers and come out something else.

Take the spiritual principle of tithing, for example. It doesn't make physical, worldly math-equation sense to give ten percent or more of your income away and expect to get ahead financially. But God says it makes spiritual sense. If you follow the spiritual world first, the physical world will bend and come along second. It's the same when you accept Christ as your savior. If you follow the spiritual principal first, the physical world must follow. The physical world says you're dead when you're buried in the box, but you will show up with Jesus when He gives the planet a make-over. You will live forever because God says you will, not because of a physical formula in the world. The physical and scientific world will tell you that no one lives past a buck thirty. This is a joke on the streets of heaven, like so many other 'facts' of the scientific, physical world. Don't be sucked in and become part of that joke.

Approach ten of the world's top university scholars and accountants who have no faith in Christ, and present the following statement:

"Sirs, I have two business plans that I'd like to discuss. My goal is to have greater financial security at the end of twenty years. In your opinion, which plan will allow me the best chance of reaching my financial goals, irrespective of any moral or societal good will?"

Plan "A": $100,000 per year income, with $10,000 taken from the income and put into stocks, bonds and a retirement account.

Plan "B": $100,000 per year income, with $10,000 taken from the income and given to my church.

From a numbers standpoint and the physical principals we live with, the question would be laughable to these university scholars. The money you spent to bring them together for an opinion would be wasted on a five second answer. Every one of them would say, "Plan A, where you invest a portion of your money rather than giving it away. That's the plan that will offer you more financial security for your future."

I don't see anywhere in God's Word where He says planning for your financial future is wrong or unwise, but if your plan for financial security in the future includes robbing God, it's a bad plan that won't work. You can't store up enough money to fix the problems you are going to have by living a life outside of God's blessings. Your enemy knows this, and that's why he spends so much of his time and effort working against you. His goal is to make it hard to believe and trust God with your money and your future.

When my kids were small, I spent most of my spare money to support the ministries God had entrusted to me. People always advised that I should be putting something away each month for my children's college educations. I chose to put all the extra money I had into the ministries and trust God for the future of my kid's college educations. I didn't have to do that, nor did I feel a mandate from God to do that. I wasn't sure about where I'd be in fifteen years, but I knew where God would be. To me, trusting Him with my children's education would be the smartest move. My daughter Natalie graduated with a four-year college degree in nursing. My son Zachary graduated with a four-year college degree in political science, and he just graduated from law school in Virginia Beach.

The Lord made a way for me to pay for both their educations without a college fund, and millions of people were reached for the Kingdom of God from the money that would have been sitting in that fund doing nothing. So I guess I chose wisely from heaven's perspective. The souls of the people who were saved through the funding of churches and missions work didn't need to be sacrificed in order for my kids to get a college education. God made things happen in a way that both were taken care of.

You can choose what you want to do with what's been given to you but you can't choose what you want to do with what is not yours. Squirrel away money for a college fund or a rainy day or even a new boat if that's the way you want to roll but make sure the squirrel is taking from what is yours (the 90%) and you're not taking Gods money (the 10%) to do it.

> *Remember this—a farmer who plants only a few seeds will get a small crop. But the one who plants generously will get a generous crop.* (2 Corinthians 9:6, NLT)

If you understand anything about farming you know that one seed doesn't only produce one more seed. It's up to you to decide how many seeds you want to plant over the ten percent tithe, but the ten percent is not yours to decide with.

I encourage anyone who is struggling with the concept of sowing and reaping, seed time and harvest, to go and eat a watermelon. Take every seed from that watermelon and plant them in their back yard. Sometime during the summer when you're stumbling through the backyard looking for a clear path to the swimming pool, the concept of giving and receiving from God should start to become a little clearer.

God's Word says that trusting Him will result in greater financial security. What it boils down to is this: Who are you going to believe, God or man? What you can't see or what you can see? Spiritual or physical principles?

> *For we live by believing and not by seeing.* (2 Corinthians 5:7, NLT)

It's scary to believe in what God says when you can't see the physical proof, but that's what faith is. The truth is, you'll have a much better future following the King's way, because His future for you is much better than any future you can plan. Get rid of the things that stand between you and God and don't listen to the doubters who want to rob you of your faith. There are many benefits to following the Lord, and many people receiving those benefits to prove it's true.

> *Therefore, since we are surrounded by such a huge crowd of witnesses to the life of faith, let us strip off every weight that slows us down, especially the sin that so easily trips us up. And let us run with endurance the race God has set before us.* (Hebrews 12:1, NLT)

When the Hummer car first came out they were a really hot item. I found one in Walnut Creek at a dealer and went right over and bought it that morning. I decided to take it for a drive over the Bay Bridge into San Francisco and stop by the San Francisco Rescue Mission and see how the director, Roger Huang, was doing. I had donated thirty or forty grand the year before and they were still in pretty bad shape financially.

The Rescue Mission is in the Tenderloin of SF, and they care for the people there in the name of Jesus Christ with the primary focus being one of saving souls. Of course that's a problem for most of the governmental authorities. Preaching the gospel precludes the Mission from receiving any government funds, and many Christian people don't care to support the homeless. Most folks feel like it's the homeless guys' fault instead of Satan's fault. They fail to see that Satan is the cause of these people's condition, and God wants them saved and the damage undone.

I had lunch with Roger and his wife Maite, and they explained their dire financial circumstances. I gave them another twenty grand to help out, but figured they would eventually succumb to the financial pressures and go under unless God intervened. The mounting debt and problems they faced were too much for them to continue much longer. They needed a complete restructuring of their operation and more people to support them. They needed someone with better skills than me, and more money than I had.

I drove back to Sonoma across the Golden Gate Bridge, enjoying the clear sunny day and the way the water glistened around Alcatraz Island, all the way across the channel to the beautiful skyline of San Francisco. There were hundreds of beautiful sailboats on the bay tacking one way or the other, and every other car that passed me on the bridge seemed to be a BMW or Mercedes. I was making my way back home to the secluded hills of Sonoma after spending two hours in the darkest corner of this beautiful city. Most people never see that area, but I couldn't get the picture of the people lying in the street out of my mind. The Tenderloin is a forgotten place with forgotten people. I couldn't stop thinking, "It shouldn't be that way!" How could so many fortunate people be living so near with so much, and be willing to give so little?

I shook off the thoughts of Roger and the people of the Tenderloin as I passed through the vineyards and rolling hills of home. After all, I was involved in helping other ministries in addition to City Impact and the Rescue Mission. I'd given them all I could. There was nothing more I could do.

The next morning at 7:00 a.m., I pulled up to the bakery and coffee shop on the square in Sonoma and was just about to open the door of the Hummer when the presence of the Holy Spirit arrested my motion. I stopped what I was doing and looked around. There was nothing near me except the birds fluttering around in the trees. I sat there for a second not feeling a particularly powerful abiding presence of God, but more like a 'passing by' presence. Then He spoke to me and said, "The Rescue Mission is not going to be able to stay in existence."

I said, "I know, Lord."

Then the Lord said, "I don't want them to cease from existence on the earth."

"Lord," I replied, "what can I do about that?"

And then He said to me, "I sent you there to keep

them from going under."

So I asked, "What can I do about that? What does that look like from a financial prospective and commitment from me?"

God said, "$200,000."

I thought about the number for a second, and then said, "Lord, that's all I have. I only have $210,000 in the bank. The mission is going in the hole $20,000 every month, so that will last for about ten months. Then neither of us will have any money, me or the Mission."

Then the Lord said, "That's okay, I'll take care of the money. Trust Me. I want you to help rebuild the Mission and keep it intact."

I thought about that for a few seconds and then said, "Okay Lord." And I opened my door and headed into the bakery.

As soon as I opened the door of the café a contractor friend of mine, Cam, came over and said, "I was hoping to see you here this morning, Benny Boy!"

I shook his hand and asked him what was going on and he explained to me that he had a friend he wanted me to meet. The guy was a Vietnam vet and in real estate, and that he had a great piece of land for sale that he thought I could develop or sell. Cam had just come from an early morning meeting at the guy's office. He was at the bakery to grab a cup of coffee and wanted to head right back over to the office while he was still there. I said okay and altered my plans for the morning to go meet the Vietnam vet real estate man.

As we were driving to the office in Cam's truck he told me about his latest fishing trip, but I wasn't really listening. I was deep in thought about the $200,000 and the Rescue Mission, and what kind of responsibility that was. I was humbled by the fact that God would trust me with something so important to Him, and I guess His presence was still around me because I was having a hard time fighting back the tears of gratitude. The truth is, when you've messed up a few times and get another chance to work for Jesus, it is a humbling experience. Cam looked at me as we were getting out of the truck and said "Hey man, are you alright?" I said "I'm good, it's just been awhile since I've been fishing." We both started to laugh as we walked across the gravel parking lot, and I told Cam I'd explain the tears to him later.

As we walked into the office I was wondering if the Lord would move so fast as to bring me a deal five minutes after I said I would help the Mission. It seemed pretty improbable, but I figured I'd meet the guy and see where this rabbit trail would lead.

Cam introduced me to Chris. We shook hands and talked about the weather and so on for a few minutes. Then I asked him what project he had. Chris got up and went over to a table in his office and brought some plans back. As soon as he unrolled the plans on his desk and I saw the boundaries and the owner's name on the blueprints I started to silently laugh to myself. This property that was for sale was a joke! It was one of those properties that had been on the market for so long you couldn't read the phone number on the faded crooked sign that had been out front for five years.

I was just about to tell the guys thanks for wasting my time in a polite way and leave, when the Spirit said to me, "Be careful." So instead of excusing myself and leaving his office, I listened to his pitch on the property, which I had already heard from other realtors over the years.

This was a great piece of real estate, only four blocks from the Sonoma Square that you could build thirty executive homes on. Unfortunately the property was landlocked without an adequate easement to access it from the main road. The neighbor who owned the property next door controlled the access, and would not grant an access easement to this place. That made the property worthless from a development standpoint, which is why the property had been for sale for so long. I knew several agents and developers who'd tried to convince the neighbor to sell or grant an easement over the years. The guy wouldn't budge.

When Chris finished his pitch I figured there must be something about the property I didn't know, or the Holy Spirit wouldn't have told me to be careful about ending the meeting. The price of the property had been reduced from a $1.5 million to $1 million, which was still twice what it was worth if it couldn't be subdivided. I told Chris to write up an offer for $990,000 and make it a thirty day contingent offer, subject to my ability to obtain an easement from the neighbor to access the property. I gave him a deposit check for $5,000 to open escrow, and then took the plans with me back to the bakery with Cam.

Cam dropped me off at the Hummer and I decided to take a drive four blocks west and see if I could catch the owner of the neighboring property. I figured I may as well find out right up front if there was a way to develop this property, and either move on it or walk away. I was still feeling the presence of the Holy Spirit, and it's a great feeling walking into the unknown with God walking beside you. There are endless possibilities with God, and the feelings of anticipation and excitement are only known by those whose futures are uncertain. So many people dread an unknown future. They try desperately to secure all the perimeters because the future scares them. God says in Jeremiah 29:11 that He knows our future and it's not anything for us to be afraid of.

I knew the land owner's name and had met him briefly a few times, but I doubted if he'd remember me. Bob had an old hay barn on his property that had been there for years and now looked out of place with the surrounding developments. A restaurant was squeezed in on the front side of the barn and houses on the other side, but behind Bob's barn was a vacant five-acre parcel that I had just put in an offer to buy.

I parked in front of Bob's locked gate and then walked down the gravel driveway towards the old barn. When I was about a hundred feet from the barn I heard a voice speak from a little shaded grove off to my left. "Hardister." I looked over and saw Bob, a kindly looking old man with a wide brim sitting on a weathered old bench. He had two twigs in one hands and a pocket knife in the other. He looked down at what he was doing with the twigs for a moment and then back up at me.

"Hardister," he said, "that is a name the town of Sonoma should be very proud of. I know your brother Mike and your dad Don. The Hardister family has been in Sonoma fifty years and they are all honest hard working people. And you're Ben Hardister, the real estate Hardister, and I guess you're here to talk to me about that driveway easement."

I nodded. "Bob, I appreciate your kind words about my family, and yes I am here to talk to you about that driveway easement."

"Well then," he said, "come on over here and have a seat."

I walked over and sat on the old gray bench next to him and he adjusted his hat and glasses then turned to get a better look at me close up. "Do you know anything about horticulture?" I told him I didn't know much and he asked, "Would you like to know something about horticulture?"

"Sure."

"Would you like a glass of iced tea?"

I said, "Sure," again.

He reached down and grabbed a pitcher and a glass, and he poured me some iced tea while he explained how to graft one tree to another and why people would do such a thing. The two twigs in his hands were branches from a plum tree and an apricot tree, I think, and he talked and demonstrated the technique of grafting and mending these two trees together for an hour or better until I could do a graft putting the two trees together by myself without his help.

After I had finished putting the rubber bands successfully on my last graft job and finished my tea, Bob said to me, "Ben, I'm going to tell you the same thing I told all those other fellas that came out here looking for a driveway easement. It's not going to happen. I don't want a bunch of neighbors breathing down on my barn and all the noise that comes with them, and I don't care how much money you offer."

I said, "Bob I can appreciate your point of view but how about if I had a way to make your land more enjoyable and protect your privacy at the same time?"

"How can you do that?"

While he'd been teaching me horticulture, I'd looked around at the peace and beauty of the place and I came up with the plan. I went out to the truck and got the map of the properties, and we laid them out on an old parts table. The property line to the vacant five-acre neighboring property was only a few feet from Bob's barn. I drew a line 100 feet out from the barn onto the other property and 400 feet long. That took about an acre or so out of the property I was buying.

Then I turned to Bob and said, "I'll give you this acre of land right next to your barn and plant it in olive trees, complete with irrigation. You'll have a buffer from anything that anyone does next door and the enjoyment of a beautiful olive grove forever. All you have to do is agree to give me a fifty foot road easement across the bottom of your property into mine."

Bob had both his palms down on the map leaning over and looking at my drawing for a minute or two, and then he looked up at me over the top of his glasses. "How come nobody else ever offered me that?"

I shrugged. "I don't know. Maybe they were greedy and wanted to build thirty houses instead of only building twenty. Or maybe they just didn't think of it."

"Nah." Bob shook his head. "They were greedy."

We talked about the spacing of the trees and various other things until noon and then I asked if I could buy him lunch. We went to lunch on the square and Bob told me all kinds of things about my home town that I never knew. He was a walking history book. Bob had been the mayor in town a few times over the years, and he was a historian on all things Sonoma. Each summer at our annual Vintage Festival he dressed the part of General Vallejo, and he always walked in the parade dressed in the period costume with his lamb chop sideburns.

After lunch we went to my office and I drew up a contract with me giving a guarantee to survey and record a one-acre lot line adjustment in his favor. In return he guaranteed to grant a fifty-foot road access easement to me. I had the document notarized and Bob back to his barn by three o'clock.

When I got back to my office I called a custom home builder in Walnut Creek that I knew had looked at the property and was interested in it. I explained to him that one acre was being given to Bob as part of the deal, and told him I had a signed easement agreement that would allow the construction of twenty homes, not thirty. He was amazed that Bob had signed an easement agreement and wanted to see the original document, a polite way of saying he didn't believe I actually had a valid agreement.

I drove to Walnut Creek to meet with him and go over the map and requirements of the agreement. By eight o'clock we had a deal for him to buy the property for $1,500,000 with escrow closing in 30 days.

The next morning when I showed up at the bakery for coffee it occurred to me that a lot had transpired in the last 24 hours since the Lord told me to trust Him. I had spent five grand and made five hundred grand in one day. I actually didn't get paid for 30 days, but that's still a pretty good return.

I am firmly convinced that if I had brushed the Lord's voice off that morning and not agreed to be His answer to the Rescue Mission's prayers, my friend Cam would not have been at the bakery waiting for me. I would have never met the Vietnam Vet Realtor Chris or the Horticulturist Ex-Mayor Bob. Every time you commit your path to God and trust Him, you are thrust forward into your destiny and a life of faith that honors God and furthers His Kingdom.

Take delight in the Lord, and he will give you your heart's desires. Commit everything you do to the Lord. Trust him, and he will help you. (Psalm 37:4-6, NLT)

I worked at City Impact and the San Francisco Rescue Mission every Thursday for over a year with labor and money. On the last Friday of the month I brought businessmen from around the Bay Area to tour the facility, have lunch, and ask for their help. City Impact and the San Francisco Rescue Mission did not vanished from the face of the earth, and they have many vibrant ministries including a Christian school, church, youth outreach, Adopt-A-Building, food kitchens, thrift shop, recovery programs, and a medical care facility. They feed tens of thousands of people a year. One of the greatest ministries that remains and continues to grow is their volunteer ministry. Over 8,000 people a year from a dozen denominations travel to the Inner City Tenderloin to stay at City Impact for a day or a week. From youth groups to seniors, they come by the thousands to minister to those in need, and they find themselves being ministered to at the same time. When a person bends down to help someone else, God bends down to help them.

I played only a small part to keep the Mission alive and going. Then other men stepped up and joined in to guarantee their success. One man or woman who trusts God with their actions can make a difference and challenge others to get engaged. Nobody wanted to fight the Philistines until David cut off Goliath's head, and then everybody joined in. Be the one who honors God by your faith in action and others will join in the battle with you.

How many places will the Lord take you if you trust and believe in Him? How many people and ministries are crying out for help, and God has planned for you to be His answer to them? You don't want to find out the answer to that question when you're in Heaven looking back and it's too late to do anything about it. Listen for the Lord's voice and have courage to act when He speaks. Your destiny is worth it. If you've been on the wrong path, thinking that faith without honoring God is an acceptable way to live, turn it around. There are people who are worth loving and people who are worth saving who will never see Jesus until they see you.

8 • Venezuela

Many times when the Lord is working in your life, you don't have the slightest inkling of what He is doing. He doesn't need to check in with us first, because He is the Master and we are the servants. Masters aren't required to check with the opinions of their servants before they do something.

Don't think you always have to hear God's voice before you do something. If it is in your heart to please God, He will always be near you. His presence and guidance will intensify as you move forward with faith in Him, regardless of whether it's your idea or His. The Holy Spirit abides in every believer so they don't need to be instructed to do things to bring glory to God—it's a natural desire.

God did not tell David to fight Goliath. David's job was to deliver bread to his brother and then come back home. Fighting Goliath to glorify God was David's idea, and he picked up some nice gifts along the way. God showed him how to win as soon as he discarded man's opinion and weapons in order to embrace God's voice and trust Him with the outcome. When David took the initiative and moved forward, God was with him.

We can do the same thing because God is an unchanging God. Is there a situation you're facing that you feel like challenging for godly reasons? You shouldn't hesitate just because you haven't heard God's voice directly instructing you to move forward. As long as your motive is to please and glorify God, have at it! He will stand with you in the fight.

We should be looking for a way to engage the enemy and fight to advance the kingdom, and not looking for a way to get off the battlefield. We can do over and above what God has asked us to do if we want to. Why shouldn't we? He does over and above for us. If someone you loved asked you to wash their car, would it be so strange for you to think consider vacuuming the interior too? It's a natural thing to want to do more for those you love. I find it peculiar that so many people are looking for the bare minimum they can get by with in giving to the Lord.

My wife Karen and I were invited by friends to a small village in Barquisimeto, Venezuela to help finish building a Bible college for a missionary friend named David. I'd never been to Venezuela and we stayed there for a week with a few dozen other people who had all invested their time and money to make this college a reality. When I heard about the needs of the Bible school and asked God about it, He told me to go and help finish the school. God defined our mission. We were very much like David in the Bible, who had a defined mission from his dad to deliver food to his brother on the battlefield and then come back home.

After working all week in Barquisimeto, our part

of the project was done, but before going back home David had arranged for a group of us to go marlin fishing at the banks of La Guairá off the coast of Caracas. We caught a flight early in the morning, planning to fish all day and then have dinner that night with our wives before flying home the next day.

As we flew into Caracas you could see whitecaps all across the ocean, and the plane was being knocked around by a pretty strong wind. When we arrived at the dock it was blowing thirty knots as we loaded the fifty-foot charter boat. We motored out of the harbor and the waves began crashing over the fly bridge as soon as we cleared the breakwater. The boat was a smoky diesel, so I was thirty feet in the air on the fly bridge with the captain to breathe the fresh ocean air. I didn't mind being splashed with occasional salt water because it was a warm day in South America.

The boat didn't make very good time against the wind and waves. About an hour into the trip, David came up the metal ladder to the fly bridge to talk about turning around. He was a nice shade of green and told us most of the guys on board were sick. We could have come about and headed back to port but something was driving us further out, and I wasn't sure what it was. Normally with a sick crew we would have just ended the trip, but we continued pushing forward to the banks of La Guairá.

When the day started, it didn't seem like God was directing us to the banks of La Guairá, or that He had any specific task for us to accomplish. As far as I could tell we were just a bunch of *amigos* going out to try and reel in a marlin, but something was brewing below the boat in the depths of the sea where we couldn't see.

When we finally got to the fishing site I didn't want to torture the guys anymore so I yelled down to David, "Let's just throw out a line for a few minutes and troll to see if the Lord has a fish for us. If not we'll pull up and head down wind home." It was difficult to keep the boat stabilized on any kind of track, and David's father Stan and I were the only ones with rods in the water because we were the only ones that weren't sick. I figured we'd give it ten minutes and that would be it.

Suddenly after only a few minutes Stan's line took off and I yelled, "Fish on!" The fish pulled for a minute or two and then broke water off the port side. She was a beauty, a big sail fish maybe two hundred pounds. She danced across the water like a Russian ballerina! The guys down in the boat's cabin moaned, "Praise God," and I don't think it was because Stan hooked such a nice fish; it was because they knew we'd be going home soon.

Stan fought the fish for maybe fifteen minutes to get it alongside boat. It was a gorgeous fish with a high sail and long bill, and it thrashed against the boat. I was leaning over the side with the deck mate trying to release the fish from the steel hook in its mouth when, abruptly, it stretched itself completely straight and became dead still. I exchanged a puzzled look with the captain up on the fly deck. He didn't speak English and I didn't speak Spanish, but it didn't matter; the look in our eyes spoke volumes to each other. Something wasn't right, this fish was still alive, but it just quit as though it were stunned by something.

I cautiously reached down to remove the hook as the deck mate held the line. All of a sudden the fish started to coil and bend itself into a U, bill to tail, away from the boat. It was so powerful that there was nothing either of us could do to control it, so we stepped back. When the fish was completely bent with its bill almost touching its tail, it thrust itself straight with great force and threw all of its guts and insides out of its mouth and onto the water. The next instant it was dead, just floating there! I looked at the captain and said, "Whoa!" The rest of the crew made their way to the side of boat and looked down at the dead fish with its insides tangled all around the bill, and nobody could figure out what had just happened.

I looked up to the captain and yelled, "What's going on, man?" He just knelt down on one knee and started doing the Catholic cross thing. Stan and I tried to describe to the rest of the crew what had just transpired. I was shouting over the windy ocean and the voice of the captain, who was yelling something in Spanish about *Santa Maria*. It was chaos, the captain freaking out, the guys all getting sick over the stern, the boat tossing and pounding against the giant waves...and a big dead fish slamming the free board.

David, who spoke Spanish, talked to the captain for a minute and then came back and told me that the fish had committed suicide. I said "What!?" I couldn't help but laugh, and said, "I know there's a lot of sick guys on this boat that might want to commit suicide, but why would this fish do it?"

David told me the captain had heard of fish doing this before but had never actually seen it. The man told David it was an act of God, and he was clearly shook up by the sight of it all.

In Venezuela it is illegal to keep game fish, and there are steep fine and jail time for those who do.

We decided to take a picture of the dead fish so we wouldn't get sideways with the law, and then chopped it up for meat and put it into several big ice chests. We arrived back at the dock in the early afternoon with two large ice chests loaded with fresh sailfish. David knew a guy in the mountains above Caracas named Juan who was running a drug rehab program and could probably use the meat. We decided to go see Juan.

It was about a thirty minute drive into the mountains and when we arrived at the rehab camp, it was nothing but cardboard huts and plastic roofs held up with tree limbs. They had a gathering area beneath a large tarp tied in some trees, with a big two-foot round pot of boiling water over an open flame beneath. The camp was only on about fifty feet wide, running along the edge of a cliff. From there it fell straight down a thousand feet to a small creek at the bottom. That creek was their only water source. They had to walk down a winding trail to the bottom of the cliff, fill containers, and then walk them all the way back up to the top.

The guy who ran the camp, Juan, was a unique man. He had been a drug dealer in the Golden Triangle until he got shot up on the streets of Venezuela and was left for dead. He had an encounter with Jesus while lying in a pool of his own blood in the gutter. During the time he was hanging between life and death, the Lord spoke to Juan and told him He was going to spare him so he could save others from the life of drugs and crime. Juan accepted Christ as his savior, and when he left the hospital some time later he began taking guys off the street and telling them about Jesus. The day we showed up Juan had about seventy guys living there.

Juan lost one of his legs in the gun battle ordeal that almost took his life two years earlier and now here he was, running this rehab camp in the jungle with one leg and a makeshift crutch. All of the men were very emotional and each of them was carrying a small dog-eared Bible. There was an excitement inside these guys at that camp, they were hugging each other and going from hut to hut spreading the news that we had arrived with fresh fish meat. Looking at their reaction to our fish meat, a person would have thought somebody had just come by and given them a million dollars. The men at this camp only ate when God supplied the food. Juan had no support or backing from any organizations or churches and neither did anyone else. They were wholly dependent on God for survival.

They all gathered around the giant pot of boiling water and Juan addressed us in Spanish, and David interpreted. All of their food supplies had run out. That morning Juan asked God how he was going to feed the men, and the Lord told him that He was going to bring them fresh fish that day. Based on his faith in what the Lord had told him, Juan sent several men down to the river to fetch water to boil in preparation for the fish. The men had walked the long trail down to the river three times. They had completely boiled the water down to nothing twice, and they were on the third pot of water when we showed up with a hundred pounds of fish filet! After the men finished eating there was enough fish left over for them to barter and trade for other food for the rest of the week.

There was something about Juan and the camp

that bothered me. God had just brought a fish up from the deep that offered its life to feed these men. I had witnessed it with my own eyes, and yet it looked like no one cared about them at all. What were these guys doing in leaky cardboard huts? I went over to the edge of the camp to sit and talk to Juan for a while, with David interpreting. This camp had nothing to do with me or my instructions from God. My task in Venezuela was to finish the Bible college in Barquisimeto. I had done that, but I had some unanswered questions about this place. What was the enemy doing, holding these guys down so tight to the ground?

After talking with Juan and David for a half hour, I was thinking that God wouldn't abide by the situation at this camp. Something needed to be done about it. This man Juan was doing God's work, and it didn't seem right that they were living in cardboard shacks. I asked them why we couldn't get some land and build a warehouse or something with some showers and maybe plant a garden. Juan said that land was very expensive in Venezuela and that you needed a lawyer to buy land. I told him that Jesus had access to a lot of money, enough to buy some land and a lawyer.

The next month my missionary pal David went back and found twenty acres of land for $50,000 U.S. Even though it had no water and no creeks, the Lord told him it was the right parcel to buy. I flew back to Caracas with the cash to buy it. When I got there David had already started clearing the land with all seventy guys swinging machetes. There was no water and no way of getting water because they don't have water drilling rigs out there, but they pressed forward with only the Word of the Lord that said this was the land to buy.

The twenty-acre parcel was a sloping hillside that got steeper at the top, and it was wall to wall jungle. They have poisonous snakes there they call "two steps." The locals say they call them that because when you get bit and take two steps you die. On the third day of clearing jungle up the hill and killing two step snakes along the way, one of the guys came running down the hill yelling his head off, "*Patron*! *Patron*!" It looked like somebody had finally gotten bit.

The men had been killing snakes and making a pile of them, which they burned at the end of every day. When David reached the top of the hill everyone was standing in a circle at the edge of the clearing. One of the workers swung his machete into the foliage and hit something with a large metal clang. Upon closer inspection they discovered a huge rusted steel pipe hidden in the thick of the jungle, running across the top of the land. The pipe turned out to be the main line that supplied Caracas with water from a reservoir miles away.

Nobody knew there was access to a water line on that land. There were no maps to show where these lines ran, at least none that we saw. David knew because he listened to God, and God knows everything. No matter how much God knows, He can't share it with you unless you have the faith to hear Him. He can't help you find your way and destiny in Him if you won't trust Him and move forward.

David kept expanding the camp, buying more property and constructing more buildings, until the ministry got so big that they needed an induction house. The induction house was to be a place where a dozen or more men could stay under medical supervision while they were dealing with the physical effect of coming down off dope. There were so many guys at the camp now that throwing detoxing addicts in with the guys who were clean was causing problems. David called me and told me about the need. They had to have $50,000 U.S. to buy the induction house. I agreed to find the money and get down there to buy the house as soon as possible.

A week later David and Juan met me at the Caracas airport. We went to David's house had some coffee and talked about the great things God was doing there. Juan told me that the relapse rate for the men in the program was less than five percent. This is unheard of anywhere in the world for secular treatment programs, and I knew it was the presence of God there that was changing men's lives.

After we talked for a while we met with some believers for dinner and I listened to them talk in Spanish for several hours. Once in a while David would lean over and explain to me what they were saying, so I followed the conversation the best I could. I love listening to people talk about Jesus when they have a passion for Him in any language, even if I can only understand a little. It seems strange to me that so many Christian people in the United States want to talk about anything *but* Jesus. If you're playing golf, hunting or just having coffee, they don't want to talk about Jesus. They change the subject as soon as they can when He comes up. They'll talk for hours about sports, cars, houses or vacations, but Jesus isn't something they dwell on. It's really different when you talk to Christians in poor countries, probably because Jesus is all they have.

David, Juan and I went to negotiate the sale of the induction house at 11:30 at night. It was the time the seller wanted to meet so we headed up to a neighborhood just outside La Vega, which is a pretty bad neighborhood. It was raining cats and dogs and very dark because there are no street lights in these kinds of places. As we traveled a few blocks higher up the hill and deeper into the abyss, there were bonfires on almost every block. The light from the fires cast a dim orange and yellow glow through the streets onto the face of the buildings. The air held a pungent smelling smoke swirling around from burning tires, and it mixed with the smell of rotting garbage and raw sewage to create an aroma all of its own. I couldn't believe we were buying a house here for fifty grand.

We stopped in front of a four-story orange stucco building that was built into the side of the hill. "This is it," David said and then he and Juan wanted to pray. I sat in the jalopy of a car while they prayed, listening to the drum roll of rain on the roof and looking at the depravation of man all around me. The streets were cluttered with hookers and dope addicts shuffling around, trying to find a buck in this toxic fumed hell hole. It amazed me to realize that Jesus loved every one of them. As David and Juan continued to pray I began to feel the pain the Lord felt for these lost souls. The reality of His love began to sink in as I felt the awesome presence of the Holy Spirit descending on us.

We met the seller inside this house that resembled the Winchester Mystery House because it had rooms and little halls going off in every direction. The seller said he wanted $350,000 U.S. and I almost fell on the floor! I've been in a few hard negotiations before but never to lower the price seven hundred percent. After several hours he agreed to take $65,000 U.S .which was $15,000 more than I had planned to spend.

When the negotiations were finished and we got back down to the street everything looked the same. Nobody had gone home and there were probably more people than before. Apparently the people in that place go twenty-four hours a day, like a dirty and broken version of Las Vegas.

On Sunday David and Juan had to preach, somewhere so a missionary friend of David's named Gary gave me a ride to the airport. Gary was a great guy and like most people who have dedicated their life to serving God, he had a passion for the lost and Jesus. On the way to the airport Gary drove by a postage stamp-sized lot, probably around twelve hundred square feet, in downtown Caracas next to a fifty-story government building. He told me that a million people a day walked by that tiny lot and that someday he was going to build an outreach there.

At the airport, we met a friend of his for lunch, a Venezuelan preacher, and we all sat down to eat before I boarded my plane. The two of them were very involved in a conversation, talking away in Spanish, and I was starting to think about home and my family. I felt good about buying the induction house, even though it was $15,000 more than I had planned to spend. I figured God would cover me on the added expense, and after all, I was through spending money in Venezuela for a while. I was in a financial bind at home and really needed God to replace what I had already spent right away.

As I ate something occurred to me about that small lot. I thought, "Man, if a million people a day walked past every day, just think of all the people who could be saved. Why wouldn't God take that land for Himself and further His Kingdom right in the middle of town?"

How much would they need to buy that land? After a few minutes of running numbers in my head and bouncing the thoughts and comparisons between residential values versus commercial values, a number popped in my head. "Ninety thousand." My first response was, "You don't have that much left in the bank." My stomach started to turn a little as I thought about the ramifications of what was coming.

My total available cash in the bank when David called and said they needed an induction house had been $110,000. I'd figured if I spent $50,000 on the induction house, I'd have enough left to cover my financial commitments for two or three months. Not much wiggle room. I'd need to get something out of the financial pipeline quickly to survive. I figured the Lord would send a deal and bless me, the way He always had before. So I'd felt pretty comfortable making the commitment to David for $50,000. I'd taken a step of faith into the dark when I agreed to spend $65,000.

This number of $90,000 floated around in my head until I began to think that I was pushing this thing too far. Maybe I should back off a little. I didn't even know this preacher Gary, and what he was doing didn't have anything to do with the reason I was sent to Venezuela. I had already done what I was supposed to do, and had actually gone over and above by fifteen grand.

While I was sitting there with all these thoughts about how bad it feels when you can't pay your bills, I began to feel the presence of fear. I immediately knew something was going on because fear was trying to get a foothold in me. I started to sweat and it wasn't that hot.

Then I realized that I didn't even know how much money Gary needed to buy that lot. He'd never said. I started to think that maybe I'd manufactured the ninety thousand number in my own mind. All these questions rolled around in my head, with the enemy's help of course. "What is wrong with you Ben? Do you need to be broke to be happy? Why are you manufacturing a battle that doesn't exist? Why are you getting in the middle of something you aren't a part of?" Then the enemy started to use Scripture on me. "You don't have enough money, and going into debt is not scriptural. The Bible says a righteous man leaves an inheritance for his children. There is safety in a multitude of council, and you haven't talked to anybody."

Isn't it amazing how many scriptures people can find to justify doing nothing? There are a lot more scriptures in the Bible that deal with going into the battle than staying out, but most people don't notice those. They are not looking for a way to get in, but a way to stay out.

This attack went on for a couple of minutes and then it dawned on me. "Why not just ask the preacher how much he needs and put an end to this mental conversation? If he says the right number, you're on the right track. If he says the wrong number you'll know it's just you."

I interrupted the conversation and asked, "Hey

Gary, how much do you need to buy that lot downtown?"

He casually replied, "Ninety thousand."

It was like the number exploded and echoed in my ears and pulsed through the rest my body! Now I knew what I suppose to do, but I would need God's power to step over my fear to accomplish it. I am and will always be a sinner as long as I am in this body. My mind is subject to sin, making me do the things I don't want to do and keeping me from doing the things I want to do.

I don't really understand myself, for I want to do what is right, but I don't do it. Instead, I do what I hate. (Romans 7:15, NLT)

As much as I wanted to move forward with His Word to me, there were still lingering questions. I needed help and courage from Jesus to pull this off now that the battle line had been drawn. I was either going to be a hunting dog or a fluffy dog and it was my call to make. I could start the fight by writing a check, but there was no way I could finish it alone.

I reached down below the table into my bag to get my checkbook and as I was bent down below the table I asked, "Jesus are you sure about this?"

I heard His response as clear as day. "Trust Me, You can trust Me."

The two preachers had gone back to their conversation. They had no idea what battle was taking place in me. I wrote a check for $90,000 and slid it across the table, saying, "You fill in the name of the ministry that's buying the lot, but don't try and cash this check until next Friday. I've got to move some things around to make that check good."

The preachers looked at me dumbfounded. They had not asked for my help at all, let alone give them the entire amount they needed. There was a lot of praising God and thanks mixed with tears, but I made it clear to them that I was only a postman. The contents of the envelope (or the check) were from God Himself, so they ought to be thanking God and not me.

About an hour later as I sat on the plane staring at the clouds below me, I felt the Spirit and the angels outside the window flying beside the plane. The battle for men's souls had intensified. I knew that my fate was tied to my faith in Him, and my fate was to bring Him honor.

I tried to get some sleep on the trip home, but thoughts of doubt circled, trying to gain access to my mind. In the midst of this, Jesus spoke to me again.

"Trust Me, you can trust Me."

His voice in my heart and His presence around me was enough to shoot the doubt birds down, and I slept all the way to San Francisco.

When I got back to my office the next day there were several messages from my civil engineer Steve in Santa Rosa. When I called him he wouldn't talk about what he wanted on the phone, but asked me to come to his office right away because he had something to show me. I figured it was bad news. Why else wouldn't he tell me over the phone? I drove right over to face the music.

Steve had some maps out on the drafting table in his office. He handed me a copy of a very old hand-drawn map with some scrawled details and a civil engineer's stamp from many years before. "Do you know what that is?"

"No, what is it," I asked.

Steve began to explain to me that while he was doing the lot line adjustment and researching the county records back to the 1800's, he found this obscure document that had been recorded years earlier. He had been working on this project for several months and neither of us knew the document existed. What Steve found was a deed that showed a five-acre parcel inside the parcel that I still owned, and was keeping. I'd sold the other thirty-seven acre parcel as part of this lot line adjustment, and the five acres was hidden inside the parcel I kept.

I asked Steve what this deed meant, and as he walked around his drafting table to hand me the plans he said, "What this means is you had two parcels. You sold one, but you still have two parcels."

We both started laughing. "What's the parcel worth?" Steve asked

"Probably a couple million bucks," I said.

I wanted to make sure the deed would hold up to the planning department's scrutiny and that the parcel was legal, and he said he'd already confirmed it with the county planning staff. He had the project plans all prepared with fresh stamps. All I had to do was go over to the county and file them.

As I was heading out the door Steve asked me, "What were you doing in South America?"

I grinned. "I was on a mission for God, like a Blues Brothers thing."

Steve said, "I believe it," and we both laughed as I left his office.

I walked across the parking lot with the plans in my hand in kind of a daze. As I was opening the door to my truck Jesus spoke to me. "See, I told you that you could trust Me."

I squeezed the plans in my hand and fell to one knee between the parked cars and began to weep. God's Spirit rolled over me again and again as I leaned my head against my truck tire, humbled in His presence. It wasn't the money that cracked me; the money was good but that wasn't what burst my heart open in gratitude. It was the fact that Jesus loved me enough to plow the road in front of me, and that His eyes were upon me. I was so unworthy and had done so many things that I couldn't take back, and yet He still steadied my hand for the battle. He still backed me up when I stepped out on nothing but faith in Him.

I know He loves me, and I know I can trust Him. It's not only because I've read it; it's because I've lived it. God has proved Himself to me over and over again. He fills my cup 'till it overflows, and He has secured my destiny for down the road.

You can trust Jesus. His plan is sublime. It doesn't matter if it's $90 or $90 million. Answer the phone when it rings in your heart and honor God by trusting Him.

I got a hard money loan against my real estate to cover the check I wrote Gary back in Venezuela but by week's end I had a buyer for my new five-acre parcel for $1.7 million so paying the ninety thousand dollar loan back and meeting my office expenses that I was sweating about a week earlier was no longer a problem. That $90,000 and my looming monthly bills that appeared so big and fearful while sitting at the lunch table in Venezuela a week earlier looked the same as Goliath after God and David got through with him—dead, with his head cut off!

9 • India

Your financial position doesn't always dictate what you can do and cannot do for God. It seems strange, but sometimes God wants to use you when you're broke and not so much when you're flush. Maybe it has something to do with being humble and totally trusting God when you have nothing. When folks are flush, they tend to have the attitude that they're doing God a favor.

I had just come back from Uganda, Africa and spent my last twenty grand helping a missionary preacher named Joab finish his school and orphanage in Kabale. I went with five guys who had put in $20,000 each to finish the project. I wasn't expecting to do anything more that year at home or anywhere on the planet, because most of my funds were gone and the projects I was working on for income were quite a ways out in the future.

A few weeks after getting home from Africa I was sitting in church listening to a missionary from India talk about the needs in Kolkota. He said they were trying to build a nursing school to train and give ac-creditation to two hundred nurses a year who would then be able to carry the gospel and healing to millions of people. The building they wanted to buy was $600,000 and the remodel was going to take another $300,000. The missionary was hoping to raise a down payment of ten percent from churches where he was scheduled to speak. It sounded like a swell idea, but it had nothing to do with me. I was tapped and was already doing my thing in Africa. We were supposed to return to Africa the next year to buy some land for a farm that would feed the kids at the school and orphanage, and I was concentrating on making the money to help cover that.

After church while I was walking my wife to the car, the Lord spoke to me and told me that He wanted me and my farming partner Gary to pay the whole cost of the building, $600,000. That was $300,000 each! My wife asked me where we were having lunch and I told her someplace special. We just started driving east. I needed some time to think and my head was swimming with God's new instructions. How could this be? How could this possibly be God telling me to do something like that? I thought I had been faithful to Uganda. Now when I needed my funds replenished for my own bills and to finish what we started in Africa, I was getting blown out of the water. Give $300,000 to India? I had $300 in the bank.

I asked the Lord how and when He wanted me to do this. He said, "Next year at this time."

Oh, I thought, *that's not so bad. God can do anything in a year. Plus, Jesus may come back before then and I won't have to worry about it.* The thought made me laugh.

The wheels of my brain started turning. I had

multiple types of projects that might be able to turn a profit like that. Suddenly I realized that my wife was speaking to me in a louder than usual voice. She had been trying to get my attention asking where we were going for lunch because we had driven ten miles out of town into the middle of farm country and there were no restaurants for miles. I had been so transfixed on my conversation with the Holy Spirit that I didn't realize where we were. I turned the car around and pointed it back towards town.

My wife asked, "What is wrong with you?" I figured I'd better let her know what was going on, so I told her the whole story. She looked at me and said, "What do you think Gary is going to say about this?" I said, "Let's go over after lunch and find out."

So we drove over to Gary's house and sat on his patio with him and the missionary, Wayne. Turns out he and the missionary were old friends, and the guy had gone to Gary's home for lunch after church.

We talked for about five minutes and then Gary said, "Hey partner, I have a bombshell for you."

He thought he had a bombshell for me? Just wait until I dropped mine on him!

He said, "I really think we should give Wayne the $60,000 he needs for the down payment on that building. The congregation gave him almost nothing. What do you think?"

I started laughing and said, "I think I have your bombshell beat. The Lord told me we were supposed to give $600,000 and pay for the whole building!"

We both started laughing, while Wayne just sat there watching us. He didn't know what to say.

After discussing the situation, we agreed that we should follow the voice of God and pledge $600,000.

My reasoning was this: what difference does it make if it was $6 million? We didn't have any money to give anyway. God would either come through with what was needed or He wouldn't, and we were willing to say that He would. I stood up from the table and shook Gary's hand, and then looked across the table at Wayne. "Preacher we'll be there in a year with the cash, so tie the building up."

The next day I left our house in Modesto to meet with some engineers who were working on one of my projects. As I drove my truck through the valley I couldn't help but notice what a beautiful time of year it was. All the trees were green and full, and the irrigation canals roared with fresh water from the reservoirs in the Sierra Nevada Mountains. The temperature was 75 degrees at six in the morning. It gets hot in the valley by the afternoon but it's the combination of heat, soil and lots of water that makes the central valley the world's leader in almond production. My thoughts were on the Lord. I was grateful for being able to live in such a nice place, and I was grateful that He was letting me be a part of helping those who didn't live in such a nice place.

When I arrived at the engineer's office, they had the plans all prepared for the project we were submitting to the county Board of Supervisors. I went over the plans in detail. Maybe this deal would help me get part of what was needed for India. I wasn't pushed for money on the India deal just yet. After all, I had a whole year to find the money for that, but my bills were due and I was feeling that pressure right up front and personal.

I had already met with the supervisor who was in charge over the district I was working in and gone over my plans with him. He'd assured me that he was behind the project. (I still have the email.) When I arrived at the hearing in the board chambers I was expecting a routine approval of my project because there was no public opposition, which is rare for any land development project. The only objections were coming from the planning department, but they usually find a reason to object to something. I think they believe it's their job to work against developers instead of helping them. I wasn't worried about the planning department because they work under the supervisors and have to do what they say, and I had already received the supervisor's support.

When my project came up, I sat and listened to one of the supervisors, a crazy little guy who was grandstanding about Ag land being taken for residential land, I really didn't pay much attention to what he was saying. The project involved taking only eight acres from a 620 acre Ag parcel, so his objections didn't make any sense. The overall impact was minimal and the only one who spoke at the public meeting was a neighbor who owned a thousand acres next door, and he spoke in favor of the project.

When it finally came time for the supervisor who'd supported my project to speak, he started waffling. He talked about heritage and grass or cows or something, and then he said he was in agreement with the little crazy guy. I couldn't believe what I was hearing. He was speaking against my project! A few minutes later they all voted to deny the project, and there was nothing I could do. You can't appeal a Board of Supervisors decision without going to court, and I didn't want to do that.

I rolled up my plans and took my file folder and

left the board chambers, marveling at what a fiasco this thing turned out to be. As I crossed the lobby a man approached and introduced himself as one of the neighbors who owned 1,000 acres next to my project. His name was Leonard. I shook his hand and he said, "Mr. Hardister, I drove all the way from Gilroy just to meet you tonight." I thought it was kind of strange that an 80-year-old man would drive so far at night to meet me. Gilroy was about a two hour drive away. I asked Leonard what he had come all that way to see me about. He said, "I've heard good things about you and decided that you should be the one who buys my land. I've got to sell it because of some family complications and I want to sell it to you."

He told me that the land was due north and contiguous to my project. He explained that the land didn't have sufficient water or soils types to grow orchards, and that he wanted to sell the ranch as grazing land for $2,800 per acre, or $2,800,000. Then he said that he wanted a $100,000 deposit and didn't want to close escrow or transfer title to the land until after the first of January for tax reasons.

I didn't have $100,000 to put down on his ranch, and I sure didn't have access to $2.8 million to buy it, but I figured I had at least a week to find a hundred grand and then five or six months to come up with the rest. I wasn't sure if the Lord had sent this guy to me so I could do something with this land or not, but if I didn't take a stab at it I'd never find out.

The problem I had up front—beyond the fact of having no money—was the price. Top dollar for grazing land was $1,500 per acre. Leonard was asking $1.3 million more than the land was worth. I didn't mention that fact at the time, and agreed to fly over to Gilroy the next day to discuss the deal. I needed to get home and find out if this was from God or not. I needed to talk to Jesus about it.

The next morning I pulled out some maps to outline the property and I prayed for guidance. The only Word I heard from God was, "Trust Me." He didn't tell me to buy or not to buy the land, just, "Trust Me." I figured the way to trust Him was to move forward until I couldn't move forward anymore. I couldn't see how backing away was trusting God, so I decided to give it a go.

I guess if you have all the resources to do whatever you want, it must be a little harder to hear from God or get directions from Him. I've never really had that luxury so I can't say for sure. If you don't need God's help and He doesn't have to open any doors or tear down any walls, then you can just move at your own pace and according to your own desires. It seems like it would be difficult sorting out your desires from His. So you actually may be in a better position with nothing than the person with everything. Don't waste your enviable position of desperately needing God versus the person who serves at their leisure by doing nothing.

I drove out to the land to have a look before flying to Gilroy. Parts of the property had a lot of rock, and it was a mile farther from the river than another property I was working on in the area that did have water. I met a neighbor, a guy named Virgil, who owned a thousand acres with an old windmill that drew water up for his cattle. He told me the water from the windmill and a few small reservoirs were sufficient for the cattle, but he didn't think there was enough water in the ground to support an orchard.

He and his wife's family had owned the ranch for more than 100 years, so I figured he must know what he was talking about.

A good almond orchard needs four to five acre feet of water per acre, and in this case that would equal four or five wells of 2,500 GPM (gallons per minute) each. I asked Virgil what he thought the GPM would be out there if a deep Ag well was drilled and he said, "Not more than 600 gallons per minute, but you never know until you drill." The part about "not knowing" caught my attention. No one knows what God will do until they trust Him and try.

> Bring all the tithes into the storehouse so there will be enough food in my Temple. If you do," says the Lord of Heaven's Armies, "I will open the windows of heaven for you. I will pour out a blessing so great you won't have enough room to take it in! Try it! Put me to the test! (Malachi 3:10, NLT)

If this land deal was from God I needed to trust Him and move forward. I asked Virgil if he had ever attempted to drill a deep Ag well and he said they had not because the water they had was sufficient for cattle.

I met Leonard that afternoon at the Gilroy airport with an offer in hand and a hot check that had to be covered in three days. I decided to give Leonard what he wanted for the land, even though the price was almost double what it was worth as grazing land. If I could find water and the soil checked out, I could get from $6,000 to $10,000 per acre. I didn't want to deprive Leonard of a blessing too. If the Holy Spirit could lead me to water on this ranch there would be enough money for both of us to be blessed. After getting signatures on the offer I flew back home to find a hundred grand and within three days. I scrapped together enough money to cover the check and open escrow.

The next week Gary and I met the well driller to schedule the work of drilling a test well. When the well man saw the map and location of the property he said that drilling a test well would probably be a waste of money. He'd drilled wells on property off Sonora Road and there was nothing down there. He said the most water we'd probably hit was 600 GPM. Sonora Road was behind Leonard's land to the north. The well driller explained that the further you get from the river and the closer you get to the hills, the worse the water got.

The nice part about being involved in projects for the Lord is that it changes your perspective on success and failure. If God sends you down to the store for a loaf of bread, He will make a way for you to pay for it. When you're going down for your own loaf of bread it's a different story. I like working on stuff that God sends me to buy. Gary and I were on our way to buy a loaf of bread that looked like a building in Kolkata India.

Gary had a guy who used copper rods bent into an "L" shape to try and locate water. The process has a lot of different names and one of them is actually called "divining water." We took the guy out there and he walked around the thousand acres for a couple days. The way it works is the copper in the rods react to the chemistry in a person's body, and they turn inward towards his body when he walks over a large deposit of water below. Most college folks that are way smarter than we are like to spend hundreds of thousands of dollars to have geological maps prepared, but their success rate for locating a good well is not as high as ours.

We located four spots where we thought there might be good water. There was only one spot on the southern end of the property closest to the river and the other three were almost a mile north towards the hills, closer to where people say there is no water.

We moved the well drilling rigs in and decided to go with the location closest to the river first. Based on what we were told, that would give us the best chance of finding water. As the rig started drilling I knew it was going to be a long day or two of waiting. We were anticipating going down five to six hundred feet. Each time the drill got thirty or forty feet deeper it had to stop and add another length to the bit. Slowly but surely we were making our way through the crust of the earth.

Sometime around two or three o'clock in the afternoon the drill stopped turning. The rig operator jumped down from the platform into the mud around the hole. He reached with both hands into the pile of sand around the bit to see what kind of minerals and materials were coming up to the surface from below. The operator turned around to face us with a big handful of soil and yelled at us over the roar of the big diesel engines, "Black sand! This is a really good sign!" We knew he was right; black sand meant we were now coming to the forefront of possibly finding very good water. Black sand was common to some of the better water strata in the area. The rig operator put on another steel extension and went back to drilling. Shortly afterwards, there was water everywhere!

For some reason I wasn't that exited. I guess it's because I knew there was water down there. I believed the Lord sent us to the right spot, and we were just proving it to the rest of the world.

That well tested out at 2,400 GPM and as we moved farther from the river where the water was supposed to be worse, it got better with each well. The last well drilled was the farthest from the river and the closest to the dry wells on Sonora Road. It was the best yet at over 3,000 GPM. The further we went from where man said there might be water, and the closer we went to where God showed us there *was* water, the better and stronger the water got.

Within a few weeks we started testing the soil for suitability to sustain an orchard. The tests came back positive for nutrients to support an almond orchard, and what was lacking in the soil could be brought up to snuff with the addition of some good ol' chicken manure. I now had land that was worth two or three times more than what I was paying for it, and began to see a clear path ahead of me for the funding of that loaf of bread in India.

The land I was buying had the most beautiful lake I had ever seen. It was tucked between the hills and ran the distance of the canyons for about a mile. There was a dam a hundred feet high on the north end that was built around 1900. The water to fill the dam flowed in from the local water district through a ten foot underground canal that came in from a larger lake up in the Sierras. The water didn't go with the land because the land wasn't part of the water district and that's why we had to drill wells, but the owner could hunt and fish in the lake.

Fifteen years earlier I had a small pond and a duck blind in Sonoma. I lost them when I got divorced and I lost my way serving the Lord. This new lake had three duck blinds and it was twenty times bigger than the old pond I used to have. I drove up the hill above the lake with my son Zack and showed him a bird's eye view of the lake. He said, "Man, Dad! It's incredible!" I asked him if he thought this lake was better than the one we had before and he said, "Are you kidding me!?" I told him it was our lake and that it was a gift from God.

The lake was on the northwest corner of the property so I decided to sell nine hundred of the thousand-acre ranch and keep the lake with a hundred acres. I was able to make good on my commitment to India almost a year to the day from when the Lord told me to give them $300,000. I had millions in real estate assets but no cash when I heard the voice of the Lord, and I watched the crash of 2007-2008 take almost all of my net worth. Yet during the hardest economic times I have ever seen, God sustained me and made it possible for me to meet the needs in India. There was even a half-million left over to meet the needs of three other ministries that year.

God told me to trust Him and I did. He protected me from a complete collapse of the economy that followed this land deal and He sustained me with very little income for four years and then I was given over one and a half million dollars for the lake property that I kept.

You prepare a table before me in the presence of my enemies. You anoint my head with oil; my cup overflows. (Psalm 23:5, NIV)

10 • BC Island

Blessings and destiny are missed when circumstances are interpreted wrongly.

You've heard it said that God controls everything. He does, but He also has an enemy that is always trying to thwart His plans. In the end God has the final say, and that is evident from reading the Bible. In this chapter I want to discuss a concept I believe will help someone who may be wrongly interpreting the events around them, and thereby missing God's plan. In this book I've written about self-deception, because it is the one thing you can't recover from until it's confronted and dealt with. This story of British Columbia describes a sure-fire method of staying in the game until it's over.

I have a litmus test I try and use to keep myself square, because we all sell ourselves on a concept of what is right or wrong from time to time. When the Lord gives me a task to accomplish and trouble arises, I ask myself this question: if I was working to complete this task for myself and it meant $500,000 in my bank account, would I quit now? If I answer that question honestly, I'll keep going ninety-nine percent of the time.

God gave me the idea of this litmus test. I want to make sure I'm not selling myself on the idea that God's work is as important to me as the work I do for myself, if it really isn't. To believe that something *is* when it *isn't* is self-deception.

I started asking myself the litmus test question for everything I did for the Lord, from witnessing to people to working on missions projects, and it really helped to ensure I gave the Lord my best effort. Not just thinking and saying I was, but really doing it.

I am acutely aware of the fact that I can sell myself on ideas for something that I want to do, as well as sell myself on ideas of *not* doing something that I don't want to do. I have watched many people bend the will of God to match their own desires. It's is a recipe for spending time in the desert and I'm not talking about Palm Springs.

My missionary friend, Wayne, asked me to speak at a men's conference on an island in British Columbia. I really didn't want to go. I don't speak much, and I try to stay away from that as much as I can. I had already decided I wasn't going to the island when I used my litmus test, "What if it was a business deal and I was making a half million bucks?" The test straightened me right out. I called Wayne and told him I would go.

I planned to fly my plane the 800 miles from Modesto to British Columbia, which would be about a four and a half hour flight. Once we were there a cab was supposed to take me to the dock to catch a businessman's yacht for another four-hour ride to the Island. My partner, Gary, had gone to India with me so I ran a guilt trip on him and he agreed to go with me to the conference.

A few days before leaving for BC, a huge cold front blew in from Alaska that covered the whole western seaboard. My plane doesn't have de-icing equipment which, means we couldn't fly it. I started to call Wayne to tell him I was out for the speaking deal when I ran my litmus test again. "If I was going to BC to pick up a check for $500,000 would I quit now?" I reasoned with myself saying, "No, I would re-schedule the meeting and meet at a later date to close the deal and pick up the check." I was comfortable with this answer and was ready to cancel the trip again with a clear conscience.

Do you see how easy it is to sell yourself on an idea when you don't want to do something? It's just as easy to sell yourself on an idea when you *want* to do something, and that's why it is so dangerous to live without proper perspectives. You have to be willing to ask and answer honest questions of yourself.

Just as I picked up the phone to call Wayne and cancel the trip, a question came to my mind that was more difficult to answer honestly. "What if you were going to British Columbia to get a check for $500,000, and the clients were leaving tomorrow for China and not coming back? Would you quit now?" My honest answer was, "No. I'd find a way." Unless I was ready to start lying to myself I had to find a way to attend that conference. So I called an airline and bought commercial tickets for me and Gary.

On Friday I picked Gary up at 4:30 in the morning. We were to catch a small plane at 6:00 a.m., fly to BC, and arrive at the boat by early afternoon so we could be on the island in time for the 6:00 p.m.

meeting. Since we were no longer flying my plane, the plan for getting to the island was now much more difficult and time consuming.

We made the Sacramento airport with plenty of time and I was feeling pretty good about giving my best effort to make God's task a priority in action and not just words. I wasn't looking forward to traveling for fourteen hours and then having to speak that night, but I figured God wouldn't be sending me up there if it wasn't important.

As we were standing around the airport waiting to board the plane, a lady came on the loud speaker and said that our flight had been delayed for thirty minutes. Forty minutes later she said the plane would be delayed another thirty minutes. An hour later the flight was cancelled. There was no way we were going to make it to that men's conference.

I didn't have any vested interest in being on that island other than to complete a task for God. I began to think that maybe we were off on this thing. If God really wanted me up there, He could have sent a good plane. For that matter He could have delayed the storm in the first place and we could have flown my own plane. These were conditions out of my control, but they were surely within God's control so He must not need us in British Columbia after all.

I thought I had given it my very best shot. I had overcome the adversity of the weather by spending thousands on airline tickets. I had taken time away from work and left the house before dawn to make it to the airport. Now it was time to admit defeat, or at least consider that we weren't supposed to be going on this trip. What else could I do?

Gary and I entered the airport restaurant and

ordered something to drink. While I was sitting there I asked myself the litmus test question one more time. "If I was going to BC to get a check for $500,000 and the clients were leaving town tomorrow for China, would I quit now?" I'd convinced myself that I had done everything I could. I was accepting as fact that God wasn't in this plan. But if I answered the question honestly one more time, I was going to have to do something radical, drastic and expensive.

I was about ready to shrug off the radical alternative brewing in my mind when it hit me. *Somebody is trying to keep me off that island tonight. I've got to do everything I can to get there.*

Maybe that somebody who was trying to keep us off that island was counting on some fluffy dogs who would lay down for a nice pet at this point, but a good hunting dog is going to hone in and go when they smell blood. I wasn't ready to be a fluffy dog.

I told Gary to finish his drink because we had some ground to cover. He asked me what I had in mind and I told him that my buddy Jim at Sky Trek had a twin F-90 Turbo Prop that would make mincemeat out of the ice storm above us. We could fly straight into BC without having to go through Seattle. If we could get back down to Modesto and go wheels up on the F-90 by 10:00 am we could still make it to the island in time.

"Are you serious?" Gary asked.

I said, "Let's give it all we've got, pal. It looks like somebody is trying to keep us off that island. If they want a fight, a fight is what we'll give them." We both laughed as we ran from the airport to my truck to beat a path back to Modesto.

I didn't know if Jim's plane was available or if

there was a pilot to fly it, but figured we would find out on the way. If Jim didn't have a pilot then it was over. I got him on the phone while speeding down Hwy 99 and explained to him that we had to be in BC for a boat ride by the afternoon. He said he could have the plane topped off and ready to go by 10 o'clock.

We skidded up to the hanger at Jim's place and ran up the stairs of the F-90, closed the door behind us, and strapped in. The pilot spooled the turbines up and we were airborne in ten minutes, filing a flight plan while climbing out. We plowed through the ice and wind for 800 miles and made it to BC in time to catch the private boat that was waiting at the yacht harbor for us.

When we got to the dock the captain was waiting inside for us. He said he had some bad news. Apparently the weather had changed significantly the past few hours. There were small craft warnings because of the wind and waves, and it was going to be very rough. I asked if we would still make the Island by 6:00 and he said, "No, but if we're lucky maybe 7:00 or 8:00." I figured these conference meetings always have a dog and pony show for an hour or two anyway so we'd probably be okay. There wasn't any cell coverage on the island because it was in the middle of nowhere so we couldn't call and say we'd be late.

After a while it got dark and cold as the small boat made its way through the winter storm. I kept my eyes on the engine gauges as I the listened to the diesels struggle against the surge of the wind and waves. If the engines quit in the middle of this storm it was a watery grave for us, but the Lord got us through the ice storm in an airplane and I had no reason to believe He wouldn't get us through a stormy ocean. Gary and I had something to drink, held on tight, and tried to keep from getting sea sick as the waves continually washed over the top of the wheel house. The captain was a man of courage to make this crossing at night, and I appreciated his faith as he fought to keep the boat on course.

I figured Jesus didn't let the disciples go down when He rode out a storm with them and He wasn't going to let us go down either, but I did fight the nagging doubt that maybe I should have used good sense and canceled the trip before it got this bad. It's no harm and no foul to have doubt when pressing forward for the Lord. It's natural to begin to doubt when things go bad, but you have to overcome the doubt and continue to move in faith. If you stop or turn around, you're done. Hold fast to your confession of faith by your actions and the outcome will honor God.

Luke 7:28 says that the greatest prophet born was John the Baptist and yet he questioned and doubted Jesus when things went wrong for him. If John the Baptist had a time of doubt, what chance do you have to never doubt? The answer is none. It doesn't matter if you doubt for a moment or a time, the important thing is to do what John did and go to Jesus with your doubt. Then defeat it and move on.

We made the island just in time to be introduced to speak. I didn't even try to explain what all we had been through for the last sixteen hours, I just started to share the things I knew about God and what it means to serve Him. I told them that I was only a mailman, and that I had done my best to show up and deliver the mail and a message from God. It was a church conference for Christian men, but I knew there was someone who needed Jesus or the devil would never have fought so hard to keep us off that island. I would travel to the other side of the world, and I have, to see one man get saved, but I wouldn't bother crossing the street just to be somebody's entertainment. I never figured God's Word or His servants were meant for entertainment. I always try to give an altar call anywhere I speak, and after everything we'd gone through, I was praying that maybe this trip would yield one soul.

When I was finished speaking and opened the altar, there were many men who came forward for prayer. None of them came to accept Jesus as Savior. It's important to pray for people and help them and I don't have a problem with that, but I'm always looking for that lost sheep because my Master is too.

If a man has a hundred sheep and one of them wanders away, what will he do? Won't he leave the ninety-nine others on the hills and go out to search for the one that is lost? (Matthew 18:12, NLT)

After the meeting ended we walked up a hill to the bunkhouse and had I to sleep on the couch because there were no more beds. The guys running the conference didn't think we were going to make it because we were so late, so they gave our beds away. I didn't care. I was so tired all I needed for a good night's sleep was a rug on the floor. Before I got my boots off, a guy came in the bunk house and invited us to go down to the dining hall for desert time. Gary and I had not eaten a single thing all day—there wasn't even a cracker on the plane or the boat—and any kind of food sounded great. So we walked down to the dining hall by water's edge.

Gary sat with Wayne, and I chose a table with a bunch of strangers who were talking about whatever. I couldn't shake the feeling that someone there really needed to make a decision for Christ. I looked at the quiet guy who was sitting on my right and asked, "What's your deal?"

He looked puzzled. "What do you mean?"

So I asked him again, "What's your deal?"

He replied, "I don't understand what you mean by that."

I angled my chair around toward him. "What's your deal? Have you made up your mind yet?"

"About what?"

"Have you made up your mind yet on whether or not you want to go to hell?" The man just stared at me like I had just kicked him where it hurts. He didn't say anything, so I asked, "What's your name?"

"My name is Theopolous," he said, "but my friends call me Theo."

"I'll call you Theopolous because you aren't my friend," I said. "Well, what's it going to be, Theopolous, have you made up your mind?"

The guy sat there for a minute, looking at the table, and then he said, "Yeah, I've made up my mind, and I don't think I want to go to hell."

I asked what he was doing there and he told me that he was from a neighboring island and that he was invited over for the weekend by a friend. It turns out Theopolous was probably the only guy on the island who wasn't saved, and he told me that he had never before heard anybody talk about God in a way that made Him sound real. We prayed together and Theopolous accepted Jesus as his Savior while sitting at the table that night. I got him a Bible to read before heading up to the bunkhouse couch and some sleep.

The next morning I told Wayne if it was all the same to him we'd like to leave that morning instead of the next day on Sunday. I'm not much for seminars and I'd pretty much said all I had to say the night before. Wayne told us that would fine, so Gary and I headed for the boat right after breakfast, before the wind started to howl. My buddy Gary never complained that I put him through hell to get to this island, and he was as grateful to the Lord as I was that God used us to bring someone into the kingdom. My good friends and I have a motto that goes like this: if you go, we go. Gary is the epitome of that motto. I think Jesus was the originator of the motto, and we all just follow His example with each other.

While we were heading down to the dock Theopolous came running down from above, yelling, "Ben, wait a minute!"

We were getting ready to push off so I asked the captain to hold up, and then met up with Theopolous on the dock. "What can I do for you Theo?"

A huge smile came across his face. "You called me Theo."

"Yeah, man, you're my friend." We laughed and I gave him hug.

We talked for a few minutes and he asked me a couple of questions about the Lord. Then he said, "I have a plan I'd like to run by you and see if you think it will work."

"Let's hear it, Theo."

Theo told me if the woman he was living with

was not the devil she was a close relative. He said all of his friends drank a lot and between them and the woman, he wasn't sure he could make it following Jesus. His plan was to move his stuff out of the house while his bad girl was at work, quit his job and move to another town where he had a job offer. He said he was going to read his Bible and pray every day before he went to work and every night when he got home. When he finished telling me his plan he grabbed my arm and asked, "Do you think I'll make it Ben?"

I said, "Theo there's no way you won't make it. That is a great plan!"

I shook his hand and gave him another hug, then jumped on the boat. While we were pulling away from the dock I yelled at him above the sound of the engines, "Theo, if these guys up here don't take care of you I'm coming back and I'll whip all of them!" We both laughed as the boat motored away from the dock towards the open water.

I went into the cabin and Gary gave me a cup of coffee, and then I went back outside into the cold winter air to sit on a bench behind the wheel house. I watched Theo standing on the dock with his Bible in his hand until he disappeared in the distance behind us, and I thought how much God loved Theo. I felt the presence of the Holy Spirit as the boat rocked its way through the waves, taking us back home, and I prayed that Theo would make it.

Three years later I saw Wayne in Modesto and he had just come back from the yearly conference the church had on the island. He told me he had a message from somebody at the conference for me. The message was this: "Tell Ben that I made it."

"Who was is from?" I asked and Wayne said, "A

guy named Theo."

Theo had made it, how great is that?

So who was the trip for, Theo or me? The answer is—it was for both of us. I needed a blessing and Theo needed to get saved. Jesus wanted a lost sheep home and He wanted to show me one more time that I could trust him.

To me it didn't seem like that trip took great faith. Others have been much harder. But it took great perspective. I continue to learn from the Master the things He wants me to know. You need faith and perspective to reach your destiny in Christ. He is willing to give you both if you ask Him.

The trip to the island cost me $13,000 and it was worth every penny. It's God's money. I am the servant, which means I'm not in control of where He spends His money.

Every year my friend Tom, a computer guy who lives in San Jose, pays for a bunch of words on the Internet that one might use to search for God. When a person clicks on a word that he has bought, they are routed to a giant live website where people are sitting in front of computers, ready to lead someone to Christ. I was visiting him in San Jose and he told me hundreds of thousands of people from all over the world were saved every year through this ministry. I was blown away by his ideas and his faith, and I asked him how much his operational costs were? Tom is a really smart guy and he knew exactly what his costs were. He told me they had factored the cost against each person who accepted Christ as their Savior, and it was pennies per soul saved. I figured that I was probably the gas guzzler of the kingdom, coming in at $13,000 per soul. I need to spend more time with

Tom.

When I left for the island my bank account was dry (again) and I was the last guy who could afford a $13,000 plane ride. I had been working on a deal selling some land to a development group, and I just couldn't get them to close on the deal. A few weeks after I returned from the island the buyers had a change of heart and decided to close on the land. My net on the deal was $500,000. This was the same number that I used in my litmus test to give me the proper prospective that sent me to BC! I don't believe in coincidences, and I'm fully convinced it was God putting an exclamation point on the lesson He'd taught me about self-deception and putting forth my best effort.

I have nothing to do with the way things have been set up. God doesn't need my help to bless me any more than water needs help to flow downhill or dirt needs help to grow a seed. It's just what they do here on this planet. God set things up the way they are when He made this place.

It's not a great secret that everything in this world is set up on sowing and reaping, seed time and harvest. You can trace everything and everybody to this principal. The past, present and future of all people and nations on the earth are tied to this principal. You can't escape it any more than you can escape gravity. If you want to change how things are in your life and you have dreams for your future, take a closer look at how and what you are sowing. You can choose a faith that honors God with your actions, or choose a faith of words without action that honors no one. It's up to you. You can choose to be a fluffy dog with all the right words in a cozy pew or you can choose to be a hunting dog who sits at the feet of his Master waiting to be turned loose to bring that lost soul back to Him. Choose wisely.

Epilogue

J ust because you're in a dire situation or going through a tough time, you're not necessarily out of the will of God. Most of the time that's a good indicator that you are in the sweet spot of His will. Of course, this only applies if your way of living lines up with the Word of God. If not, the hard times are going to keep coming until God gets your attention. God will do everything He can to bring you around through circumstances, but He won't force you to do anything. God didn't create robots. He left you with a free will. It's up to you to decide when enough is enough.

When the disciples of Jesus were at death's door in the middle of the Sea of Galilee, they were in the right place, at the right time, going in the right direction with the Son of God Himself. It had been Jesus's idea to go. The disciples had been safe in the harbor, minding their own business on dry land, when Jesus decided to go for a boat ride to the other side. Jesus was leading the way.

As evening came, Jesus said to his disciples, "Let's cross to the other side of the lake." (Mark 4:35, NLT)

The disciples' immediate problems were those of life and death, which is more than most of us face in our quest to faithfully serve God. The disciples didn't do anything wrong. They were doing what they were meant to be doing. They were learning through experience Who Jesus was. What did it matter if they panicked and got it wrong at that time? They found themselves in that circumstance so they wouldn't get it wrong later, when it counted.

I used to race airplanes in Reno and I would practice flying low, fast and very close to the ground above the farm fields of Schellville. I would turn the plane upside down and fly flat out with the ground and blades of grass twenty feet below my cockpit canopy. I'd practice pushing the stick, which would thrust the airplane back up higher into the air. A pilot's natural reaction when he sees dirt is to pull. By pulling the stick, you bring your tail feathers down and that causes the plane to thrust skyward. When flying inverted, or upside down, your stick control input is backwards, so pulling the stick while flying fast and low inverted will put you in the dirt headfirst in a millisecond. Then you get to meet Jesus quickly and unannounced.

When you are flying in an air race, there might be five or six airplanes bunched up and the prop wash from the other planes can flip you over. If you follow your natural instinct when you see the dirt and pull the stick, you die. So you practice in non-race conditions. See dirt—push! See dirt—push!" until it becomes part of your instinct to push instead of pull. You spend time training so that when it counts during a race you don't make the wrong decision and fail.

Many people have failed and been discarded by their peers. That can get a guy down, but what they don't realize is that the failure was only part of the training God was giving them so they didn't fail in the future, when it really counted.

Others may think your failure at the moment is what really counts. You may believe that too, but it isn't true. I'm sure Peter thought what he was going through at that moment, walking on the water with Jesus, was the event that mattered. It wasn't. Peter probably figured for sure his denial of Jesus when the rooster crowed was the end, the ultimate failure. It wasn't. Peter was being groomed and prepared. The experience was designed to give him faith that would honor God for the road ahead. Jesus didn't mind him failing then, because He knew the experiences would keep him from failing in the future when it counted. Jesus was right. Peter didn't fail when it counted!

If a person knows that these are the last days we are living in, then they know it's time to push. A distance runner calls it the "kick," and when they're approaching the end of the race, they give it all they've got.

You are going to need the right perspective and faith in Christ to reach your destiny. Don't run from the hard experiences; run right at them. For every victory there is honor that goes to God, for it is faith in Him that *brings* that victory. Have faith in Him through your actions, get in the race, and make a difference in the world for Christ. He has plans for you. What looks like a mountain today will only be a speed bump in your rear view mirror tomorrow.

For I know the plans I have for you," says the Lord. "They are plans for good and not for disaster, to give you a future and a hope. (Jeremiah 29:11, NLT)

The greatest honor anyone can give God is to accept by faith His Son Jesus Christ as their Savior and Messiah. God did His very best by giving His very best. When you accept those efforts extended by Him on your behalf, God is honored and you become a driver on the highway to heaven. Once you have accepted Jesus Christ as your King and Savior, don't stop honoring Him. Stay on the road of faith and let your actions prove what you believe by the things you do.

And always be a dog that can hunt.

About Ben Hardister

Ben Hardister was born and raised in the Sonoma Valley of California. He has worked in real estate and related fields of business for 35 years. He is the past president and founder of the Full Gospel Businessmen's Fellowship International in Sonoma, and past President and co-founder of Prison Bible Studies, in San Quentin. Mr. Hardister was a volunteer chaplain on San Quentin's death row for ten years, and has funded the building of churches, schools, orphanages, youth centers, homeless shelters, clinics and hospitals worldwide and he is currently the chaplain of the Soldiers Of The Cross Motorcycle

Club. He and his wife Karen attend church at The House in Modesto, and reside in Sonoma and Modesto, California. They have three grown children and four grandchildren.

Mr. Hardister remains active in the planning and funding of projects to further the kingdom of God in the United States and many countries around the world, and he leads a weekly Bible study at his home in Modesto.

Contact Ben at ben.hardister@gmail.com.